NO ONE TAUGHT ME TO TANGO: MEMORIES OF ANGLO-ARGENTINA

NO ONE TAUGHT ME TO TANGO: MEMORIES OF ANGLO-ARGENTINA

TREVOR GROVE

THE **BLACK SPRING**
PRESS GROUP

First published in 2023
Eyewear Publishing, an imprint of The Black Spring Press Group
Maida Vale, London w9
United Kingdom

Cover painting Mr and Mrs Grove at the Confiteria Ideal
    by Philip Hood
Inside illustrations The author's brother, Colin Grove
Typesetting User Design, Illustration and Typesetting, UK

ISBN-13 978-1-915406-14-9

CONTENTS

SALIDA   9

CAMINITA   25

BANDONEON   43

OCHO   53

LUNFARDO   69

BALANCEO   91

GANCHO   105

SALIDA   163

Para la papirusa y los Hnos

*The hornero, or oven-bird,
of the pampas in her nest of
sun-baked mud*

*M*i Buenos Aires Querido – My Beloved Buenos Aires – is a famous tango. When I grew up there in the 1950s, in the days of President Perón and the sainted Evita, tango was the sound of the city. Twenty years on, in 1972, my father was kidnapped by urban guerrillas and held in a subterranean cell. He – and his family – feared his murder, which had been the fate of an Italian hostage not long before. Straining for clues as to the whereabouts of his 'people's prison', he heard only the occasional passing car above the soundtrack of the day-long tango music from his captors' radio. Later in that black decade, when 'to disappear' became a transitive verb, the military torturers played tangos to drown the screams of their victims. During Argentina's economic collapse in the 1990s, the despairing people of Buenos Aires found solace in the tango. It expressed a gloomy sense of identity. The sardonic Argentine writer Jorge Luis Borges had mused that perhaps this was tango's mission: to give Argentines the belief in a valiant past, in having met the demands of bravery and honour. So, it's no ordinary music, and no ordinary dance. As a teenage exile sent to be schooled in England and then as an adult living in London, I rarely heard the tango. But whenever I did, it was the trigger for instant nostalgia. As for the dance, I grew more and more regretful that no one had taught me to tango.

SALIDA

I f you are a beginner, you must begin somewhere. In skiing it is the snowplough. This stops the novice instantly careering into a tangle of arms and legs. In tango the basic eight-step routine known as the *paso basico* or *salida* has a similar purpose. True *milongueros*, the native tango-dancers of Buenos Aires, scorn the basic step. They say there is no such thing: the Argentine tango, as opposed to the robotic ballroom version, is improvised. It must spring from the heart – from the leader's response to the music and his partner's response to him.

Teachers of tango think otherwise, obviously, since if they are to earn their crust they must have something to teach. And you can't teach inspiration. So that's why, sometime back in the 1940s, they concocted the basic step, which is how novices have been taught ever since.

This is how it goes. The man leads, but his first move is backwards, on his right foot. This might appear like a surrender but is in fact a seduction. He draws his partner towards him, then slides to his left, tracing the second leg of an irregular quadrilateral. It is the woman who is now in retreat. On the fifth step she pauses, with her left foot crossed prettily over her right ankle. In another three beats, the couple are back to the position in which they started, feet together, face to face.

The manoeuvre is complete. But the dance has barely begun. In Spanish, *salida* means both start, as in a race, and exit, as in a cinema. In tango, there is no contradiction: the way out of one sequence is also the departure point for the next.

My own start was so much on the late side that I was almost at the exit before I'd begun. I was nearly 60 when I took my first tango steps, so an unkind person could say it was a *salida* in both senses. Though a keen dancer, I was immediately in difficulties. For my generation, most social dancing required a good deal of shoulder-shake and shimmy. Not tango. 'Do not jig,' said the teacher severely. 'The tango is a dance where your feet must *caress* the floor. It is a kind of walking.'

I now own a pair of supple, suede-soled tango shoes but, after years of spasmodic lessons and many nights of stumbling across crowded dance-floors, still struggle with the walking. And so far from scorning the basic step, it remains a comfort zone. Snared in some over-ambitious bit of footwork, I am prone to return to start, as in a terpsichorean board game, and set off with my partner once again in the familiar pattern of the *salida*. Only if she is excessively patient (or your wife) will a partner endure such uninventiveness for longer than a dance or two.

I should point out right away that there are certain highly civilised conventions in a tango hall. Tango is user-friendly. Singletons always find partners. Wall-flowers are unknown. The dance is the thing. A man may give a smile and a small nod of the head – *un cabeceo* – to any woman in the room. Generally, the woman will nod back and join him on the floor. It is the polite thing to do. As the music starts, they embrace. They may or may not exchange names. Most tangos are only about three minutes long and most couples, however new to each other, stay together for three dances. That is basic good manners. If things are going well, they'll carry on. If not so well, they thank each other and return to their tables. So you can see that if they flee from you after just a couple of sorties in your arms, you're not cutting the mustard.

Once upon a time I would have given the whole thing up as a bad job. If in Latin mood, I would have stuck to the samba, a much less demanding dance. The Brazilians are feverish jig-gers. But that would have been BTA, before *Tango Argentino*. This was the show that electrified Broadway and the West End in the 1980s, igniting an explosion of similar hits around the world and launching a thousand tango classes from Tokyo to Helsinki. From then on, I harboured a secret desire to learn to tango.

It was not just that the dance was bewitching. It was also because, though born in Britain, I had grown up in Buenos Aires, the birthplace of the tango. The tango and I had shared a cradle, or in my case a high-sided cot with cream-painted bars. Hearing that pulsing, plaintive music again in *Tango Argentino*, watching the couples respond to it with move-ments at once so passionate and so controlled, I was stricken first with nostalgia, then envy – finally, black indignation. Gringo I might be, but I could barbecue steak, ride a horse, speak Spanish and eat raw garlic. How come I could not tango? This was a part of my heritage too. Yet it had eluded me. Or maybe I had eluded it.

In 1997 came Sally Potter's thrilling film *The Tango Lesson*, a further spur to action. During a reception at the Argentine Embassy in London, in the presence of President Menem, who happened to be on an official visit, Sally and Pablo Veron, her leading man in both senses of the phrase, did a demonstration dance. Then spivvy little Menem himself, hair slicked, side-whiskers flared, swaggered onto the floor. Though the son of Syrian émigrés, perversely nicknamed El Turco, he moved as smoothly as a native. Surely I should get cracking, before Japanese and Finnish, not to mention Syrian Sally Potter fans swamped the dance-floors.

My wife Valerie asked: how did I want to mark my sixtieth year on earth? A few tango lessons, I ventured, then a tango tour of Buenos Aires.

I was not quite two years old when I toddled down the rattling wooden gangplank of the ss *Highland Chieftain*, 14,500 tons, and set foot in the country that was to be my home for the rest of my childhood. Who could have foretold that 57 years later this same small, Clarks-sandalled foot would be clad in a size 10 dance shoe, attempting to tango in the grimy upstairs room of an Irish pub in Tufnell Park, North London?

Philosophers of the tango (of whom there are a tiresome number) like to describe the dance as a journey of self-discovery. To see real life in the same metaphorical light,

however, one must first have lived it. The past is the only bit
of the road that can be mapped. One has been there. So if I
am to be fanciful, that was where my journey from Buenos
Aires to the upstairs room of The Boston Arms began
– on the cobbled quayside of the great port on the River
Plate.

Today there are no cargo-ships or ocean liners tying up
at the bulbous iron bollards. The docks have moved south.
Puerto Madero has become a fashionable esplanade of bars
and smoke-scented steak-houses. But then it was a place
of torrid human drama, thronged with pistol-packing
policemen, corrupt customs officials, beseeching porters,
sweating stevedores and bewildered passengers, elbowing
and bribing their way through the melée.

I picture my parents holding on to me tightly and shading
their eyes to watch the netloads of iron-bound cabin trunks
labelled Not Wanted On Voyage being craned out of the
hold and over the rails. Their past lay packed in those
trunks. Their future must have seemed almost as uncertain
as for the millions of immigrants from southern Italy and
Galicia, the Basque Country and Northern Europe who had
thronged to Argentina before and between the wars.

Well, that is a bit of an exaggeration. Most of those immigrants had been poor, single young men, desperate for work
(much like those hordes throwing themselves on southern
Europe's shores right now though, unlike them, welcomed
with open arms). Whereas my father had money in his
pocket, a job to go to and a pretty wife. Still, for both of them
it must have seemed the start of a dizzying adventure as their

taxi hurtled from the customs house into the broiling pande-
monium of the Buenos Aires traffic.

Some years later I was in a party of schoolboys shown
around the offices of the *Standard* newspaper, which had
been keeping Argentina's British community abreast of
world affairs since 1861. (It folded in 1959, leaving the field
to the almost as venerable *Buenos Aires Herald*, which lasted
until 2017, having survived years of journalistic defiance
against the military dictatorship.) One of the *Standard's*
printers showed me a block of metal which he then inked
and stamped on a sheet of paper. To my excitement, there was
a grainy image of my father in a cream suit and Panama hat,
smiling broadly, with his arm around my mother in a summer
frock. I, aged 22 months, am in a fetching pair of dungaree
shorts, sucking my fingers. The caption said something about
the new deputy general manager of the Frigorifico Anglo
meat-packing plant stepping off the boat from England with
his family. So our arrival had not gone unnoticed. That was
the first occasion I appeared in print.

It was the end of 1946. Our voyage had brought us 7,000
miles south, leaving behind a threadbare Britain shivering
through a terrible winter. Not only was rationing still in
force: in some respects it was even tougher than in war-
time, thanks to wheat shortages and a failed potato crop.
My father had been in the meat trade at Smithfield since his
teens. Then, in his twenties, he leapt at the chance to earn a
bit more (£5 a week) by working in Buenos Aires for a few
years. When war broke out he had been called back home,
deflected from joining up and co-opted to work in the

Southwards bound: mother and son aboard the Highland Chieftain

Ministry of Food for the duration. (He always said the future prime minister Harold Wilson, then a hotshot young statistician, was a colleague, though I've found no record of this). Dad's job was to help administer the rationing system. Did he enjoy the irony of this as we steamed through shoals of flying fish into the southern summer, towards a land of almost nauseating plenty?

Probably not, as he was a kind man and we had left relatives behind eking out their margarine and powdered egg. But I don't think it can have troubled him too much either. In the photo album of the trip, there are tiny black and white pictures showing him leaping gaily about the deck-tennis court in Aertex shirt and plimsolls. My mother looks equally sporting and impossibly young. She was 30, my father eight years older. It was his second marriage, something I'd always known. However, it was also hers, though I wasn't to find that out until much later in my life.

They would have continued their benign conspiracy to shield their three sons from this indelicate fact for ever, I suppose, but for my mother's younger brother, my somewhat louche, ex-Spitfire pilot Uncle Tony. One day over a pint in a Shepherd Market pub, an old haunt of his RAF days, the mischievous uncle revealed the truth about his sibling. I was then 18, but still thunderstruck to learn that the dazzling young woman in those early photographs, my mother, was not a virgin bride, as I had grown up to believe, but a divorcée and indeed an adulterer, like my dad. Their illicit courtship had begun over the washing-up in the kitchen of the small house in Rhos-on-Sea, North Wales, where my father was

Buenos Aires here we come: dad and lad on the high seas

posted for much of the war. His new love was the then wife of another Ministry of Food man. What shameless wickedness.

It would have changed nothing had I known sooner, I suppose. The photo albums were my touchstone as regards my parents' early married life. I and later my two brothers would pore over them. It was quite obvious, from those small, sharp images, gummed in place by photo-corners like miniature black pirate hats, that our parents were a reassuringly perfect couple. Whatever their previous experiences, the photographic evidence was that in that first full year of peace, sailing aboard the *Highland Chieftain* towards a new life in a new land with their almost-new baby boy, Ronnie and Lesley were touchingly happy.

I can't be sure whether I really remember anything about the voyage that isn't the product of the snaps – Brownie box camera-induced false memory syndrome. What I seem to recall to this day, however, is the spectacle of the godlike captain pacing the bridge in his whites, the Royal Mail Line's peaked cap at a jaunty angle, as he conned the ship into one or other of our ports of call. Also, being taught to swim by Chief Officer Pearce in the passengers' sea-water canvas pool, whose surface tilted alarmingly with every roll of the ship. I named my first canary Georgie, in honour of Captain George Bannister, and I remember a period when I was so scared of going into the sea, following Mr Pearce's unsuccessful lessons, that I would only do so wearing a rubber ring and Wellingtons. So perhaps these memories are authentic.

While my parents searched for somewhere to live, we roughed it at the Alvear Palace, the grandest hotel in

Buenos Aires. It was built in 1932, but its rococo airs and graces were those of pre-revolutionary France rather than an unstable 20th century South American republic. Even the sand in the pillar-borne ashtrays was freshly embossed each morning with a regal coat of arms. Do I remember what it was like to be a small boy wandering those lofty corridors and salons, while the traffic hooted incessantly outside and the ladies of the city gathered for petits fours and afternoon tea in the conservatory, fanning their powdered faces from the heat? I like to think so. But anyway my lifelong love of being at sea and staying in posh hotels suggests that the events of 1946 did plant a taste for exotic living in my infant mind.

On New Year's Day 1947 I had my second birthday. My present was an Amerindian bamboo flute. A little English boy of the period might have expected a tin drum or a penny whistle, but I fancy my parents' gift was thoughtfully chosen. It demonstrated their wish to bring me up appreciating the native culture of our new homeland. Or maybe it was the only suitable thing in the hotel gift shop. At any rate, I was reportedly very happy with the instrument. I would purse my lips and attempt to pipe on it while sitting on my potty, a level of musicianship from which I did not rise far in later life. In adolescence I played a Dolmetsch descant recorder and then a B Flat clarinet bristling with valves and levers. But not once did I manage to produce the breathy, yearning note of the Andean *quena*, a length of cane with half a dozen holes in it whose sound has haunted me ever since, as well as Simon and Garfunkel and millions of world-music fans.

Some weeks later, we moved the cabin-trunks and ourselves into a sixth-floor flat in Palermo Chico, a residential
neighbourhood of Buenos Aires pleasingly embellished with
fountains, boating ponds and patriotic statuary. The parks
were overseen by bronze or marble epauletted generals on
chargers and bare-breasted women whose loose gowns from
their shoulders did fall. After war-weary London, where my
parents and I lived for a year before heading for the far side
of the world, it must have seemed like paradise. Our quiet
street was lined with mauve-blossomed jacarandas. Parakeets
screeched in the palm-trees. Tiny humming birds hovered
among hibiscus flowers. From the balcony there was a vista
across pram-haunted parks towards the grandiose Graeco-
Roman temple which housed the university's Faculty of
Law. We could hear the distant boom of ships' sirens on the
River Plate. From half a mile away, trains trundling north on
the Ferrocarril Nacional General San Martin (built by the
British, named after the nation's Liberator, appropriated and
almost ruined by General Perón) gently rattled our windows.

But despite these reassuring sounds of 20th century
commerce and my father's big, black, newly-purchased
Chevrolet down in the garage, the ambience of the city
was still barely post-Victorian. The milkman, the green-
grocer and the baker delivered their wares by horse-drawn
cart, bringing housewives and maids scurrying downstairs
to make their purchases and myself to feed carrots to the
blinkered nags. I could mimic all the different street cries
that echoed up to us on the sixth floor: the flamenco wails
of the basket-seller-cum-bottle-collector perched on top of

his teetering wagon, the pan-pipe glissando of the itinerant knife-grinder, the come-hither cry of the ice-cream man: 'Helado Lapóniaaaa!'

For poultry, rabbits and fresh fish I would accompany my mother to the Las Heras market, whose cast-iron vaults echoed to the squawks and squeals of livestock. While she haggled with stall-holders in primitive Spanish, I would stand transfixed, watching the bloody-aproned poultryman wringing chickens' necks to order. He killed them quickly, enfolding the frantic feathers under his left arm, grasping the bird's gullet with the fingers of his right hand, just below its cackling beak. Then he'd give a sharp, nonchalant tug. Soon all flapping ceased. And the plucking began.

These close encounters with death excited and alarmed me. Clattering home on the tram with our greaseproof paper parcels of still-warm flesh, assorted giblets and hen's feet, we'd pass another sight that always gave me a disturbing thrill: the windowless, yellow-walled, castellated prison, whose grim ramparts were patrolled by policemen with machine-guns. Our cook, who liked to make my flesh creep, told me this was where the most vicious murderers were sent to rot. Today it has been pulled down and replaced by a plaza. But then, the juxtaposition of the public executions in the market and the cut-throats in the jail made shopping expeditions dreadfully alluring.

The tram-ride, squashed up against persons who might be carrying dismembered piglets home from market or visiting notorious killers in the prison, was part of the adventure. Buenos Aires in the 1940s and '50s was known to anoraks of the time as the City of Trams. There were a world-record 535 miles of rails, 3,000 tramcars and more than 12,000 staff, all amounting to a colourful and reliable urban transport system whose passing was even more regrettable than that of the Routemaster bus in London half a century later. The best of it was that in the never-ending duel between the tram and the freewheeling rubber-tyred rivals with which it shared the road-space, the tram always won. Even trolley-buses gave way.

My father soon learned that the smoothest way to drive his Chevy along the city's rumbling cobbled streets was to set his tyres in the tramlines, as all the taxi-drivers did. But just as quickly he discovered the importance of derailing before being rammed in the backside by a bell-clanging, spark-wreathed, unstoppable *tranvia*. Who needed bus-lanes when the tram was king? Looking back, I'm not sure which I preferred: co-piloting my dad as he yawed exhilaratingly along the tracks like a skier on a rutted piste, with a tram just a few feet behind him, or sitting on the hard wooden seats of the tram itself, butting everything else out of the way like a Sherman tank.

My mother and I would jump off the tram's rear platform at the corner of Avenida Las Heras and Calle Tagle. Tagle was our street, a longish one, this being a city laid out in grid formation. We were still a 15 minute walk from home. But there was a recompense, an oasis, right there on the corner, a *panaderia* whose pastries were baked in heaven – sticky *palmeras,* or pigs' ears as my mother called them, *media-lunas* (half-moons, i.e. croissants) filled with melted cheese and, best of all, small round cakelets of intense chocolatey sweetness called *miramenometoques*

– look-at-me-but-don't-touch-me's. They had to be handled with extreme care. They would disintegrate before they reached your mouth if you weren't very, very careful. My job was to get them home intact.

Our route took us past the familiar headquarters of the Automóvil Club Argentino, where I always had my hair cut among the vintage Bugattis. '*Medio-Americano, no muy corto,*' I was taught to say to the barber, which meant 'half-American, not too short'. In other words, pretty severe, but less savage than a crew-cut. Everyone in Argentina who wasn't American was anti-Yanqui in those days, as now; but the British, it seemed, at least in the matter of haircuts, only went half-way.

From the ACA we had to get across the roaring expanse of Avenida Libertador, which is as wide as an airport runway, then Figueroa Alcorta, a thoroughfare dominated then as now by crazily-driven buses. These privately-owned, over-crammed *colectivos* were in desperate competition with each other, which is why they were painted as gaily as canal boats and employed would-be Fangios to race between the stops. ('*Prohibido escupir*', 'No spitting', said the signs inside). There were no traffic lights in those days, so crossing the road was as dangerous as dodging the bulls at Pamplona. Undaunted, my mother would haul me to the other side while I nursed the cardboard box of delicacies as if it were a consignment of gel-ignite. With pride I would open it at the tea-table, seeing all the little cocoa-coloured cakes still in one piece, not a single casualty, and manoeuvre them onto a serving dish with as much care as a nuclear scientist. Proust had his *madeleines*. I have my *miramenometoques*.

CAMINITA

To say the tango is a kind of walking makes it sound easy. But that is because normally we walk without thinking about it. The moment you do give the matter your full attention, it is extraordinary how awkward the process becomes. For each of your limbs and extremities you are suddenly faced with a range of options. Take the foot: should you place it on the ground toe first, heel first or flat? What angle the ankle? How bent the knee? It is like being told that life is a kind of breathing, which is true but could lead to a panic attack if contemplated too deeply.

The *caminita*, the basic tango walk, must be smooth and relaxed. The upper body remains level, the sole of the foot skims the floor. You must not hop or skip or jump or wag your head about. At our first lesson my wife and I weren't even allowed to attempt the *salida* until we had spent half an hour doing lengths of The Boston Arms's upper room. Biljana, the Serbian tango teacher from Sarajevo, a sylph in cargo pants, walked with us. Or rather she glided along-side, her trainers padding across the beer-stained boards as stealthily as a cat's paws. We, by contrast, might have been wearing flippers.

Biljana Lipic had been recommended to us as the best tango teacher in London by our friend Clive James. Author, wit, poet and TV host, Clive was also an accomplished tango dancer. In fact, being stocky and barrel-chested, he was the ideal build to make a woman feel confident in his arms. 'Don't even try any fancy stuff,' was his sage advice. He had taken to tango when writing about Argentina for the *Observer*. On his return, he had fallen for Biljana, as did we when we entered the upper room of The Boston Arms for our first lesson. But for her radiant presence, we might have turned tail at the door. There were a few cheap chairs and tables around the walls and a primitive bar. Otherwise the room was dingy, cheerless, dirty and smelt of Jeyes fluid. Most evenings the place was called The Dome and hosted club nights of the nastiest, noisiest kind for north Londoners of our children's generation. But then on Wednesdays it became Zero Hour, named after an album by the coolest of tango-composers, Astor Piazzolla. Red cloths were draped over the shabby tables. Candles were lit. There were vases of flowers. Men unzipped their anoraks; girls got out of their puffa jackets to reveal slinky dresses or tight jeans and changed shoes into strappy high heels. The character-less room was now transformed into the nearest thing to a Buenos Aires tango salon anywhere in London.

The lessons with Biljana were an early 60th birthday present from Mrs Grove. As she once wrote: 'I knew T was that rare creature – a man who loves to dance. It was part of his appeal. For years, whenever the invitation said 'Dancing' I knew he would have to dance every dance – not just with me but with all those charming but unfortunate wives whose husbands fled to the bar. For our first 30 years, we embarrassed our young with our *Saturday Night Fever* routines, honed at Pepe Moreno's disco in 1970s Marbella, which descended into post-millennial dad dancing. We held barn dances on our silver and ruby anniversaries, where astonished guests discovered that they hadn't had such fun for years.

'But ah – the tango. Watching *Tango Argentino* and another show called *Tango Por Dos* in the 1980s, I fell in love with the soulful rhythms, the sexy dresses and the nifty foot-work. You couldn't watch and not want to try it. Who could not love a dance that started with an embrace (*el abrazo*)? If only we could master it.'

Had I known about the *salida* and the *caminita* at the age of three or four, I might have had a head start on Sally Potter and Biljana. Almost every radio station in Buenos Aires played non-stop tango music except when it was broad-casting a football match. I need only have switched on my parents' wireless in its walnut cabinet, of much the same design and not a lot smaller than a 1940s Odeon cinema, and I could have practised my steps instead of marching about with my pop-gun. The shape of our new apartment would have lent itself to this, being curiously long and narrow, with the kitchen and servants' quarters at one end, the sitting room and balcony at the other. Such was the pat-tern of middle class dwelling in those days of cheap service. Cooks and maids were consigned to cheerless tiled areas in the innermost recesses. They had tiny bedrooms, *chambres de bonne*, equipped with single iron bedsteads, while their employers enjoyed airy reception rooms, repro French or

English furniture and sunlit views across the city. To me this seemed the natural order of things, though in Britain the days of live-in staff were already gone.

My mother engaged Juan and Carmen as soon as we moved in. They were a married couple. How they made do in the iron bedstead department I can't say. Juan waited at table in a black jacket and did the housework in a long grey apron. Carmen was the cook. I remember her a lot more clearly because not only was she a fiery Latin beauty but she also sang operatic arias at the stove and smoked cigarettes over the saucepans. It was like having Maria Callas in the kitchen. Did she model herself on Bizet's heroine? Most likely, my parents boasted to their friends, for when Carmen and her husband weren't on duty at home they were members of a *claque* at the city's famous 1908 opera house, the Teatro Colón.

They knew and loved their operas. But that wasn't the main point of attending, which was that in exchange for free seats in the upper circle and indiscreet sums of money, they were ready to cheer one singer or hiss another at the top of their voices, depending on who hired them for the performance. And woe betide the innocent tenor or arrogant prima donna, newly-arrived from Covent Garden or La Scala, who failed to get a *claque* on side. Thanks to the likes of Juan and Carmen they might never be invited to sing at the Colón again.

Perhaps the power went to their heads. Maybe Carmen got to join the chorus. At any rate, they left. Whereupon enter Berta and Luisa, who were to stay with our family for the next 20 years. They were an ill-matched pair. Berta, the cook, was a large, scowling, formidably ugly woman with the wiry black hair and hook-nose of an Inca chieftain. Luisa was tiny and hunchbacked, but sweet-natured and not easily bullied. I loved them both dearly, as they loved me and later my two brothers. Once, my parents came back late from a dinner party to find Berta asleep on the floor beside my bed, like the faithful Nana in *Peter Pan*. I had been having bad dreams, she grunted, then padded back to her room in her nightgown on gnarled bare feet.

Despite her appearance, Berta was a splendid cook. Her specialities included a spicy stew of tripe, called *mondongo*, and another, *carbonada*, consisting of beef, barley, sweet-corn and fresh peaches served inside a pumpkin.

CARBONADA CRIOLLA EN ZAPALLO
Serves 6

This is a rich, spectacular dish, best eaten when there's a chill in the air. In the northern hemisphere, a good occasion to try it would be at Halloween.

Ingredients & method
- One good-sized pumpkin.
- 500g diced beef.
- Two medium onions, chopped.
- One red or green pepper, sliced.
- Half can of chopped tomatoes.
- Large sweet potato, peeled and cubed.

- Large potato, peeled and cubed.
- Two sweet-corns, sliced into 50cm rounds.
- A cup of barley.
- 800ml beef stock.
- Garlic clove, chopped. Bay leaf.
- One tsp each of oregano & ground cumin.
- Three fresh peaches, peeled, stoned and cubed; or one can sliced peaches.

1 Pre-heat oven to 375°F.
2 Cut open the lid of the pumpkin. Clean out the inside, removing and discarding seeds and strings.
3 Oil inside and out. Bake at 180°C about 50 minutes, until just tender when pierced.
4 While the pumpkin is baking, heat oil in a heavy saucepan over medium-high heat. Brown beef on all sides, then transfer it to a bowl.
5 Reduce heat to medium. Add garlic, onions, and pepper. Cook until soft, about 10–15 minutes.
6 Add beef, tomatoes, beef stock, barley and all spices.
7 Bring to a boil, then reduce heat, cover and simmer for 80 minutes.
8 Add potatoes and cook for 20 minutes. Add water if looking dry.
9 Add corn and cook another 10 minutes.
10 Spoon stew into the pumpkin, stir in peaches and bake in oven for another 30 minutes.
11 Remove from oven, season and serve.

My favourite of Berta's dishes was the Argentine version of shepherd's pie, which surely owed something to the influence of Moorish Spain, for as well as minced lamb and mashed potatoes it included olives, sultanas, cumin, cloves, garlic, and hard-boiled eggs. Here's the recipe. For variation's sake, I've attempted it in verse:

PASTEL DE PAPA

Here's how to make a Shepherd's Pie
That's good to taste and catch the eye.
Disdain just onions, spuds and meat:
Throw in some spices, something sweet.
In Argentina, migrant land,
They turn their backs on flavours bland.
So: two chopped onions, medium sized,
Slow cook until caramelised.
Now stir in your ingredient chief,
Three-quarters kilo lamb or beef –
Yes minced, of course; now start to fry
Quite gently until meat is dry.
Throw in tomatoes, chopped, one can,
Three cloves of garlic, crushed, in pan.
Two cups sultanas sweetness add
(Though there are those who'll think this mad).
Some roasted cumin seeds in stir;
And olives (green ones, I prefer),
Pitted, sliced, about a cup.
Then simmer 'til half-hour is up.

Meantime potatoes must be boiled
(But peel them first in case they're soiled).
With lots of butter, salt – then smash.
Hey presto: you have perfect mash.
Set this aside, return to stove
And sprinkle meat with buds of clove.
Now let it cool and season well:
Adjust for moisture, taste and smell.
Spoon mixture into dish that fits,
Chop six hard-boiled eggs in bits.
Then scatter over top of pie,
Spread on the mash and pile it high.
Heat up in oven, medium hot:
Pastel de Papa's what you've got.

Over time, Berta and my mother developed an impressive
Anglo-Argentine repertoire ranging from jugged hare to
pickled partridges. For pudding there was treacle tart or pan-
cakes filled with a local delicacy, a caramelised milk-and-
sugar goo called *dulce de leche*, which means milk jam (nowa-
days available as a Haagen Dazs ice cream). But since we were
on the edge of the pampas and my father was in the business,
what we mostly ate was meat.

Scarcely a day went by without everyone in the household
consuming a fillet steak as thick as your fist. I also remember
gagging over dishes of brains and slabs of liver, thought good
for a growing boy. Such was the carnivorous tendency that
there was even a special contraption, like the duck-press in
old-fashioned French restaurants, for squeezing the bloody
juice from bits of underdone beef. I drank this from a coffee

Champion sire: boy and bull at the Buenos Aires cattle show

cup, with a pinch of salt. It was so delicious I scarcely needed Berta to urge me on, saying it would make an *hombre* of me.

Such an abundance of good things pained my mother when she thought of the privations being endured 'back home'. (The British always talked about 'home' in those days, rather than 'the UK', even when they'd been settled in the country for generations.) She assuaged her guilt by waging a fierce war on waste. There was no question of leaving something on my plate for Captain Manners. Every morsel must be consumed, even if it meant sitting over my Beatrix Potter bowl of congealed tapioca for an hour or more.

My mother taught Berta to make meringues. The morning after a successful dinner party which had concluded with a great platter of these delicacies, oozing whipped cream, she congratulated Berta, then asked her, by the way, what she planned to do with the two dozen egg-yolks. Berta said, well, nothing *Señora*: I threw them down the sink. My mother was absolutely appalled and gave the uncomprehending cook a terrible dressing-down for being so wasteful. Some while later, meringues were again on the menu. My mother went out to the kitchen to thank Berta for the excellent dinner but found her groaning and looking queasy. What was wrong? *Señora*, said Berta, you told me not to throw the yolks away when I made meringues. Yes, replied my mother kindly, so what did you do with them? Well, *Señora*, said the unhappy woman, I ate them.

When they weren't working, Berta and Luisa had an alcove between the dining room and the kitchen where they would sit at a lino-covered table drinking *yerba mate* and alarming me with stories about the *hombre de la bolsa*, the old man who would take children away in his sack if they were naughty. *Mate* is the native tea that's made in a gourd and sucked up through a silver straw. Spanish colonists picked up the habit from the indigenous inhabitants centuries ago. I was never sure I liked it. The *mate* gourd is passed from hand to hand like a peace-pipe, topped up with splashes of boiling water as required. The silver mouthpiece of the *bombilla* scalded my lips and the brew itself was bitter, even when sweetened with sugar. But Berta insisted it was good for me. According to her, the gauchos, the almost mythic, footloose cattlehands of the pampas, who ate nothing but meat and would slaughter a steer for a single steak, could never have survived but for sucking down litres of *mate* round the camp fire. She was probably right. An authoritative website lists enough components in *Ilex paraguariensis* for a Gilbertian patter-song. They include cellulose, gums, dextrin, mucilage, glucose, pentose, fat substances, aromatic resin, legumin, albumin, xanthine, theophylline, caffearin, folic acid, caffeic acid, viridic acid, chlorophyll, cholesterin and essential oil. When burnt, the ashes reveal great amounts of potassium, lithium, folic, sulfuric, carbon, chloric and citric acids, beside magnesium, manganese, iron, aluminum and arsenic traces. What more could you ask of a cup of tea?

Like lots of girls escaping rural poverty, Berta and Luisa had come to Buenos Aires from villages in the north of Argentina to find work as servants, which is what they remained until the end of their lives. They never married or even had a boyfriend. Once a year they packed their cheap

Mate gourd with thermos and sugar bowl

suitcases and took 48-hour bus journeys into the interior to spend a week or two with their relatives. They would return bringing us parcels of country cakes called *alfajores* (from their name you can spot the influence of Moorish Spain again). Otherwise, they showed little interest in the outside world, except, of course, that they were both ardent Peronistas.

Peronists? One might imagine this was a bit like harbouring a couple of fascists in the home, since General Perón's brutish brand of demagoguery was closely modelled on that of his hero Mussolini. But not even my father, who took a dim view of the president, thought any the worse of Berta and Luisa for the way they voted. Every working class Argentine did the same. And after all, it was less a case of political allegiance than of idolatry, the chief object of the people's veneration being not so much the president himself as his wife, Evita.

Colonel Juan Perón, a seasoned military plotter, rose to power in 1946 on a tidal wave of support from poor urban workers. He rallied the mob from the balcony of the pink-painted seat of government, the Casa Rosada, calling them *mis descamisados*, my shirtless ones. He rewarded himself by self-promotion to general and the shirtless ones with schools, hospitals, previously unheard of welfare benefits and rousing anti-American rhetoric. He was content to let them believe all this largesse was at the instigation of his former mistress, now wife, a small-time former actress called Eva Duarte.

Her popularity was immense. If she was not regarded as co-president of the republic, it was only because she was more like its queen. The childless Evita was a combination of film star, class warrior and the Virgin Mary. She outshone the bourgeois opera-goers by wearing couture silk and diamond tiaras to the Colón. Everyone, my parents included, would stand as she entered the theatre's presidential box. But she was even more fervently applauded when she wore mink to visit an orphanage. Forty years on, when Princess Diana toured Buenos Aires in 1995, comforting the afflicted and dispensing sweetness, everyone in the city caught the echoes: Laidi Di (pronounced Dee), as they called her, was a second coming. Viva Evita. Long live Evita.

Actually Evita died in July 1952, of cancer. She was just 33. Over the following weeks, millions queued to pay their respects to her embalmed body as it lay in state. Sixteen people died and thousands were injured in the hysterical crush. Did Berta and Luisa join the mourners? I think they did. I know they were weeping around the flat for days. I was pretty stricken myself, aged all of seven years old. Since it was dangerous to say anything critical about Perón or his wife, and my parents were always very guarded, I got my politics from Berta and Luisa. I grew up in the shadow of enormous roadside posters showing the faces of brilliantined, raven-haired Juan and blonde-bunned Evita, above a slogan which read: *Los únicos privilegiados son los niños* – the only privileged ones are the children. So naturally they got my vote. I was distressed that the more endearing of this pair of deities was dead. Besides, from the age of six I had been attending an Argentine primary school where each day began with the singing of the national anthem and there were pictures of the Peróns in every classroom. Obviously I was a Peronist, even though as a Viyella wearer I couldn't count myself a shirtless one.

The desire to be thought an authentic Argentine despite my fair hair and gringo birth was troubling from the start. Children of the Raj and colonial Africa know the problem. I wanted to belong to the place I lived in, not some fogbound island an ocean away which my parents insisted on calling 'home'. There was an ordeal I particularly resented when out and about with my mother. Matrons would advance on me in shops and cafés, total strangers, and pinch my cheek,

exclaiming *'Ay, que rubio!'* – what a blondie. This was painful
and humiliating. At school it was easier to blend in with the
locals: like all state-school pupils, we wore white cotton coats
over our clothes so we all looked like miniature lab techni-
cians. Every Friday morning I joined the crocodile to walk
hand in hand to the nearby Catholic church for confession.
But as a Protestant I was not allowed into the gothic sentry
box where my school-fellows knelt one by one to tell the
priest their sins. I had to stay put in my pew. It seemed inex-
plicably unfair that I was the only one deprived of absolution,
even though I'd have been stumped to conjure up a single
Hail Mary's worth of evil-doing.

From a tender age I was scornful of my mother's Spanish.
Her verbs were all in the infinitive. *'Por favor cocinar huevos
para los chicos, Berta... traer las cosas para té, Luisa...'* (Please
to cook eggs for the boys... to bring the things for tea).
My brothers and I found this squirm-making. Everyone
else was enchanted. My father's Spanish was better, but still
not as fluent as my own, though obviously I'd have had a bit
of trouble talking about corned beef export tariffs to the
Minister of Agriculture, which was the sort of thing he had
to do. I picked up the language as small children do, without
a thought – from Berta and Luisa and the horse-drawn
tradesmen and other kids. In the next-door flat on the sixth
floor lived my friend Camilo. He and I played in the park
every day and listened to Tarzan on the radio. By the time
I went to school, I had no more difficulty rattling through
the Lord's Prayer or reciting patriotic verses at assembly than
I did trilling the jingle for a chocolate drink called Toddy,

which all little Tarzans liked to drink. *'Todos los Tarzanitos toman Toddy!'* Small children are parrots, though with maybe more than a parrot's understanding. The Tierra del Fuego Indian children encountered by Captain FitzRoy and Charles Darwin in the course of the Beagle's famous voyage in the 1830s picked up salty naval English within days.

Mention of Camilo reminds me I shouldn't overdo the golden childhood stuff. He'd often secretly shown me the out-of-bounds cabinet containing his father's gun collection, which I'd gaze at in awe. He can't yet have been ten years old, I think, when he walked into the study one morning to find it splattered with blood and bits of bone. His father's body lay on the floor, alongside a still-warm shotgun. To this day I remember the horror of the event and the stoical manner in which little Camilo tried to comfort his mother Dora. When I was 16 or so, back home on holiday from my school in England, it was Camilo who introduced me to the Latin code of conduct among the well-to-do when it came to matters of young manhood. He took me to a buffet dinner party where the chaps in suits and ties flirted with sensationally pretty girls in cocktail dresses. At about 11pm, the girls were escorted home. Then the young men reconvened at a less well-lit venue, put their ties in their pockets and got down to dirty dancing with a whole new bevy of dark-eyed beauties, somewhat more riskily dressed than their predecessors and decidedly less prim. The first lot were the girls one might one day marry, winked Camilo. One was not permitted to sleep with them. The second were the mistresses, present or potential. To my English public schoolboy mind, still stuck at the snog-and-fumble stage, this was unbelievably worldly. What was more, the parents of these bumptious boys positively encouraged such behaviour. I could only gape. Many years later, when I took my family on a three-week holiday to introduce them to Argentina, it was Camilo who showed them around the Boca and San Telmo, the picturesque quarters at the heart of old Buenos Aires. He had grown up to be a smiling, smoothly-bearded man, as handsome as Antonio Banderas. My wife and children thought he was adorable.

But these things were yet to come. As children Camilo and I, when it was not the Tarzan hour, grew up to a background of tango music. It emanated from the kitchen and the servants' bedrooms. It was piped six storeys up the lift-shaft from the cavernous communal garage, where gammy-legged Antonio spent his days polishing the automobiles and smoking Tuscan cigars. We were friends. He called me Trebolin. '*Dove vai, Treboliiiin?*' he'd bellow, as I headed for the park with my Dinky toys and cowboy gun, making the garage echo with his exotic version of my name. Antonio still used odd bits of Italian, though it must have been many years since he'd stepped off the boat from Naples to find his fortune in the New World. His fortune had not amounted to much. He lived alone in a small, windowless cell at the rear of the garage, where I sometimes caught a glimpse of an unmade bed, a gas-ring and a radio.

The radio, with its unvarying tango output, was a comfort maybe.

BANDONEON

Bandoneon

Y ou can play tango without the *bandoneon*. You could
have a Viennese waltz without strings. But neither would
be recognisably itself. The serpentine squeeze-box, writhing
and coiling across the player's knee, is the defining instrument of the tango. It wails like a tipsy mourner at a wake,
swoops in sudden surges of emotion, gasps in short, fierce
bursts with the urgency of love-making. Just three or four
chords from a *bandoneon* place a tune as surely in the birthplace of the tango as a bagpipe's drone says Scotland or an
accordion conjures up Montmartre.

The *bandoneon* was a 19th century button and bellows instrument developed in Germany as a more powerful version of the reedy concertina, chiefly to accompany hymns. Presumably when it reached Argentina in the mid-1880s it was in the baggage of God-fearing Lutherans, determined to preserve their own wholesome forms of worship in a predominantly Catholic land. But somehow the *bandoneon* went wildly astray. Thousands of miles from home, this pious invention found its musical apotheosis not in Sunday morning chapel but among the ungodly bars and brothels of Buenos Aires.

Tango was the music of lonely men. It sprang from the nostalgia of bachelor immigrants like Antonio who had landed on the shores of the River Plate in huge waves during the last quarter of the 19th century and the early decades of the 20th. In the course of 50 years, six and a half million people settled in Argentina. Many came from northerly climes – France, Germany, and the British Isles. According to one startling statistic, by the 1870s there were 35,000 Irish shepherds in the country. But the vast, overwhelming majority of the newcomers were from Catholic southern Europe, predominantly the poorer regions of Italy and Spain. In the city of Buenos Aires alone, the population between 1880 and 1910 sextupled to 1.3 million, making it the second largest city in the Americas after New York. And nearly all the newcomers were young, single males.

Those who settled in the capital, rather than striking off

into the interior in search of agricultural work, found themselves living in teeming dockland *barrios* already overpopulated with the urban poor as well as criminal riffraff of one kind or another. The immigrants who joined this low-life throng were packed into squalid boarding houses known as *conventillos*, sleeping a dozen to a room, where the different nationalities had to rub along as best they could. For most of these young men, their new lives must have been desperate, dangerous and bitterly disappointing.

Drink and music provided some consolation. In the evenings, after long hours butchering steers, packing hides or loading ships, the men escaped their cramped quarters by gathering on street corners and in bars. Like exiles everywhere, they played and sang about distant homelands and lost loves. At first it was in their own tongues and rhythms – musical traditions as far removed from each other as Bohemian polkas and Irish jigs. But over time, a distinctive new melting-pot music emerged, rooted in the Buenos Aires slums.

No one is completely sure of the cultural blend that produced the tango. But the basic ingredients included the Spanish *fandango*, the Cuban *habanera*, and the racy *milonga* of the pampas gauchos, which supposedly combined native Indian rhythms with the music of the earliest white settlers from Spain. The *milonga* is still danced to this day as a kind of sub-species of tango, as is the tango-waltz, plainly of northern European origin. Into this mix, the Italians must surely have thrown a pinch of the southern *tarantella* and a dash of popular opera. As for the insistent rhythm of the tango, by common consent this came from the black Africans imported by the early colonists as slaves, who evolved their own River Plate music, the *candombe*.

One must take this on trust, since modern Buenos Aires has to be one of the whitest cities in the western hemisphere. The disappearance of the black population of Argentina is a national mystery. One horribly plausible explanation is that these people were used as expendable soldiery in the genocidal campaigns against the native Indians in the 19th century, thus ensuring that the country's two prevailing racial problems cancelled each other out by mutual annihilation. These events are seldom talked about, though the gene pool does not let modern Argentines forget the vanished races altogether. When I was a schoolboy, anyone at all dark-skinned was automatically nicknamed 'Indio' or 'Negro', but always in the friendliest fashion. I, with my peeling summer nose, rather envied them.

It may be that the very term 'tango' had African origins. A favourite theory is that the slaves in what later became Argentina and Uruguay called their drums 'tambo' or 'tangó' ('compare Ibibio *tamgu,* to dance', says the *Collins English Dictionary* helpfully). Over time these words also came to mean the places where black people gathered to enjoy *candombe*. Others believe tango was simply a diminutive of fandango, while classicists point out that the Latin verb meaning 'I touch' provides an etymology both apt and suggestive.

With the music came the dance. Here again, the historians bicker. Jorge Luis Borges, Argentina's greatest writer and most exotic interpreter, much- drawn to machismo and hot-bloodedness, insisted that the tango was born in the brothels of Buenos Aires. Hence the lascivious movements, the rude titles – *El choclo* (the corn-cob), *El fierrazo* (the iron rod). This is the generally accepted version of events, supporting the wearisome cliché that tango is the vertical expression of a horizontal desire (well, maybe, but so is the fox-trot, arguably). Nevertheless, despite his eminence, Borges is not the tango's unchallenged Darwin. Other authorities argue that the origins were to be traced to perfectly ordinary and respectable dance-halls.

Well, I'm afraid this won't do. What we want with regard to the tango is loucheness, and there are plenty of reasons to think Borges was right. The influx of immigrants to Buenos Aires at the turn of the 20th century was predominantly male. In the 1850s, the population of the city was fairly balanced between men and women. But by 1914, the male populace was about 850,000, outnumbering females by more than 125,000. In the poorer barrios the ratio was still more uneven. Amidst so much surplus testosterone, prostitution thrived.

Pretty well every tango stage-show there's ever been tells the same story. The last one I saw was in Buenos Aires. It was called *Tanguera*. Typically, Act 1 crowds the stage with young migrants disembarking at the docks, singing of their hopes and fears. The backdrop in Act 2 is the façade of a brothel, a *prostíbulo*. Men mill about awaiting their turn with one of the girls inside. We are led to believe that back-street Buenos Aires brothels routinely ran to three-piece combos playing music to entertain the clients. Do we detect the embryonic rhythms of the tango? We do.

An attractive young woman emerges from the brothel.

Does the spiv in the rakish black trilby seize her tightly and step into a dance which demonstrates (a) his dominance and (b) her fiery sexuality? Sí señor. This illustrates one favourite theory of the tango: that it was an expression of the tense relationship between pimp and prostitute, he controlling and possessive, she by turns dependent and defiant.

In their frustration, some of the men watching this arousing display form couples and begin to dance together. They show off madly, each trying to outwit the other with dazzling footwork and suggestive sashays. This is another popular legend about the origins of tango – that it was largely the invention of sexually charged-up blokes impatient at having to queue for a woman. To pass the time, they put their arms around each other and developed dance steps that both mimicked human coupling and gave them a pre-coital opportunity to flaunt their prowess.

Naturally, one of these young men is a sharper dancer than his mates. Emboldened, he cuts in on the pimp in the trilby and steals his girl, whirling her into a breathtaking display of inventiveness. She responds by sliding her foot lewdly up and down his leg and performing playful back-kicks into his crotch. The infuriated pimp retaliates, swings her away for an aggressive pas-de-deux to remind her who's the boss (lots more kicks to the groin), before our hero catches her in his arms again, his superior technique silkily winning the encounter between good and evil.

Thus is another version of the dance's origins offered to the audience: the tango as a contest, where the swagger and ingenuity of the truly macho man wins the compliance of the woman, who responds by harmonising rapturously to his every move.

At this point in the show, the director may well go for the old cliché of a knife-fight between the two men, *mano a mano*, underlining the close affinity between dance and duel. The tango is not for sissies.

Eventually, the other girls bounce merrily out of the brothel doors, step over the pimp's bloodied corpse and team up with the boys who have previously been dancing with each other. Then the whole company goes into a spectacular choreographic routine of interweaving legs and flying feet. The tango has been born.

The next act generally shows how the tango spread to northern Europe and America during the first two decades of the 20th century. From the somewhat crude 'Apache' version which took bohemian Paris by storm, with its brutal stripe-shirted matelots and quailing women, via the cinema's smouldering Rudolph Valentino, the tango reached chic 1920s salons in a rage of popularity. The stiff-necked, sexually neutral movements which gave the dance its entrée into white tie and tails circles dominates ballroom tango to this day. It was (and is) a million miles from its origins in the mean streets of Buenos Aires.

But by becoming fashionable overseas, the tango won acceptability at home. It emerged from the sleazy dives of the urban under-class and found its way into respectable middle-class homes. Even the Vatican's ban on the notoriously lascivious dance was lifted after the Pope had witnessed a demonstration. The tango had come of age. Or so says popular history.

Total rot, counter those who dismiss the whole brothel-to-ballroom fable. For a start, these scholars argue, the *prostibulos* of turn-of-the-century Buenos Aires were far too shabby to lay on musicians for their clients. The only chance of hearing a tune would have been a passing barrel-organ. Second, it is plain from the sales of records and sheet-music in the early 1900s that the tango was popular with all classes. Between 1903 and 1910, there were 1,000 new records released in the city, of which a third were tangos. Of the 5,500 produced in the next ten years, more than half were tangos. Since both gramophones and pianos were expensive, it is safe to assume it was well-off folk who were buying, playing, listening and dancing to these newly-published tunes. As to the papal censure, there is no documentary evidence the Vatican lifted a ban or ever even imposed one in the first place. So much for the showbiz version of events.

Hmm. Naturally I prefer the idea of the tango as exotic national myth rather than as a mere dance like the Charleston or the cha-cha-cha. Here is Borges again, referring to two of his favourite tangos: 'As for me, I confess I cannot hear *El marne* or *Don Juan* without remembering precisely an apocryphal past, at once stoical and orgiastic, in which I have challenged and fought, only to fall finally, silently, in an obscure knife-fight.' Could one say such things about the quickstep?

Anyway, I don't think it's correct to say the tango was freed of its lower class associations from early on. If intellectuals and younger members of the bourgeoisie took it up, its subversive roots were surely part of the appeal – the rap music of its time. Between the two world wars, the most famous of all tango-singers, French-born Carlos Gardel, might be said to have tamed the tango with his lounge-lizard charm and double-breasted suits. But even Gardel remained a spiv at heart, a working class hero as authentic as Elvis or Maradona.

At any rate, it must be significant that throughout the political turmoil of 20th century Argentine politics, tango tended to thrive under populist governments and retreat when the military were in charge. Under Perón and Evita, tango was the national Muzak. In 1950 Perón decreed that 50 per cent of broadcast music should be Argentine, and most of that was tango. Which is why the largely anti-Peronist middle classes shunned it and why I and my Argentine contemporaries, nice little boys and girls, never even saw a tango danced, never mind being instructed how to do it. The very idea would have been shameful.

So I was 18 before I experienced my first live tango. I had gone home to Buenos Aires after finishing at my English boarding school and before going up to Oxford. At parties everyone was dancing the twist, which was thought very cool. But my friend Michael Combes and I were cooler still, because we were the only two people in the entire country who knew how to do a line-dance called the Madison, which had not yet reached the southern hemisphere. It was rather thrilling to be the sole importers of a new dance craze. After one impromptu Madison class, I asked whether anyone would respond with a tango demonstration. It emerged there were just two people at the party who could oblige,

Eduardo and his sister Maria Marta. They only consented after much badgering from the rest of us and even then with some embarrassment, as if knowing the steps at all were itself rather shocking. Which it was. How we applauded.

No one could have imagined that half a century later, in 2014, hundreds of people would celebrate the 78th birthday of an Argentine Pope by dancing the tango in St Peter's Square.

OCHO

The first proper figure you learn in tango is the *ocho*, which means eight. Actually for the man there isn't much learning involved. He simply has to use subtle ('Do not *yank* your partner!') movements of his torso to invite the lady to make the moves. It is she who does the fancy stuff. In the forward ocho she slides past the man's right side on her right foot, loops her left foot over her right and reverses direction until she is back facing her partner. In the backwards ocho she retreats, crossing one foot behind the other in a zigzag pattern that could be said to trace figures of eight on the dancefloor. This may not sound like much of a step, but when you see it done, you know you are watching the tango. And when you manage to do it, well, to return to a skiing analogy, it's a bit like making your first parallel turn. You're beginning to cut the rug.

(By the way, any reader who has difficulty picturing these steps should turn to Paul Pellicoro, the man who taught Al Pacino to tango in *Scent of a Woman*. His book *Paul Pellicoro on Tango*, Souvenir Press, doesn't only have helpful how-to photographs, chapters on history, showbiz, famous performers, recordings and the like, but even tells you what clothes to wear: a skirt, he confirms, may indeed have a slit.)

At the age of eight I was still at my Argentine primary school, Angel Gallardo, where we learnt to read, form our letters and write sentences by strictly old-fashioned methods. We assembled every morning in the courtyard wearing our class-concealing white pinafores to say prayers and sing anthems. On days of national celebration, of which there was an extraordinary number, including the Day of the Revolution, the Day of Independence, the Day of the Flag, the Day of the Escarapela (a blue-and-white republican rosette pinned to the lapel), the Day of the Worker, the Day of the Teacher, and even (rather impressively in those pre-ecologically-conscious times) the Day of the Tree, we took it in turns to recite patriotic verses standing on a podium. It was unthinkable that any child should have left that excellent school unable to read or write or draw an instantly recognisable picture of the little house in the northern city of Tucumán where the Declaration of Independence was signed on 9 July, 1816. I can draw it to this day.

My sensible parents had sent me to this entirely Spanish-speaking school from the age of six. My English education in those years consisted of no more than a weekly visit to a severe matron called Mrs Goodson. The first lesson Mrs Goodson taught me began unpromisingly. 'Long, long ago,' said the text-book, 'men lived in caves.' Since I already knew from my daily schooling at Angel Gallardo all about Adam and Eve, the Virgin Mary, Christopher Columbus and the founding of the Argentine republic, this seemed like a retrograde step. The only other lesson of Mrs Goodson's I remember required me to write a sentence using the words

'British Commonwealth'. She was not pleased with my offering, which was: 'I met my mother for tea in the British Commonwealth.'

As a matter of fact, where my mother and I usually had tea when we went into town, after I'd been put through some horrid experience like a visit to the dentist or a session at her dressmaker's, was the Confiteria Ideal. This was a fine old café with gilt mirrors, lofty pillars and white-aproned waiters. It was notable for ice-cream sodas and three-decker sandwiches made with soft crustless bread as thin as a communion wafer. There was a teatime orchestra which played *La Vie en Rose* and *The Blue Danube*, though never as far as I recall a tango. Yet unknown to my mother and myself, there was a dance-hall upstairs which was one of the most famous tango venues in the city – and still is, as I would find out half a century later.

At nine, I was told I was to be sent away to boarding school. This was devastating. Not even the novelty of getting my new uniform and a pair of football boots at the Buenos Aires branch of Harrods could make up for the prospective sense of loss. I was about to be removed from everything and everyone that made life sweet: home, parents, brother, Berta and Luisa, my next-door chum Camilo, my friends at Angel Gallardo and my solid-tyred bicycle, which did double-duty as a horse called Lightning. What's more, I had no idea what lay ahead. Parents are apt to forget how little of the world small children know. Both my father and mother had left their day-schools at 16 – my mother to go to RADA and enjoy a brief career as an actress, my father to don a white coat as a junior salesman in Smithfield meat market. Having risen in the world, they now thought it right to follow the English middle-class tradition, as adopted by the Anglo-Argentine community, of sending children away to private boarding establishments.

There were several in the country, modelled on British lines. The most prestigious was St George's, in a town called Quilmes, 20 km south of Buenos Aires. Since my parents had no personal experience of such places, they can only have committed me to this institution on the basis of their friends' say-so. For them, it was a known unknown, as US Defence Secretary Donald Rumsfeld would one day put it. But for me, it was an utterly unknown unknown. I remember being driven there by my stony-faced father and gently weeping mother and feeling as if I were about to be launched into outer space. Actually, it was worse than that.

My first night at St George's Preparatory School could have made a chapter in a childhood misery memoir. Soon after a supper of fatty bacon, bread and tea during which no new boy dared speak, an electric bell propelled us up to our dormitories for the night. In mine there were a dozen thin-mattressed iron bedsteads, each equipped with a small locker. At one end of the room was a single bed which belonged to the dorm captain. At the other was a zinc pail.

None of us new boys had any experience of communal living. Under the harsh ceiling lights, how could we undress and get into our pyjamas in privacy? The dilemma was resolved when the dorm captain, who couldn't have been more than ten years old, shouted an order: unless we were all in bed in eight minutes' time we would be punished. He held up a leather slipper and brought it down on his locker with a terrible whack. We leapt out of our clothes, stifling sobs, and into our night attire. There was a race to the washroom to brush teeth, etc, then a dash back to our grim little cots. Frantically, I wondered what to do about saying my prayers. Would I be thought a sissy if I knelt by my bed, like I did at home? Would I have time to reach 'God bless Mummy and Daddy and Peter and Berta and Luisa' before I received a blow from the flailing slipper?

Most of us compromised, dropping to our knees for about 15 seconds, then hurling ourselves beneath the covers. A bell went. 'Silence!' yelled the dorm captain and turned out the lights. 'From now on no one is to say a word.' We heard him slap the shoe into the palm of his hand. 'No one may leave the dormitory during the night. If you want to do pi-pi, use the bucket. Kneel down and make sure you don't miss. Now go to sleep.'

As if we could. Softly at first, then with increasing volume, each little boy began to weep. Soon the whole dorm was heaving with sobs. 'Shut up. Don't be such cry-babies,' commanded the captain. For a while there was hush, then we all began again.

It must have been about one in the morning, as I stared miserably into the darkness, face wet with tears, that I heard padding steps, followed by a thump and then the unmistakable sound of someone peeing into a metal container. Others followed. The tinkling sound changed note as the bucket began to fill. I was bursting to go, but mortified at the idea of doing so in this humiliating fashion, without even a torch to light the way. The mass pee-in went on through the night, some boys going more than once. By the time I could endure no longer and knelt down beside the bucket, I realised I had left it too late. Urine was already slopping over the top of the pail and onto the floor. My pyjama knees were soaked. The smell was vile. Crying with shame, I peed nonetheless, sending more cascades down the outside of the bucket.

Since we had barely slept all night, we were awake long before the bell for reveille sounded – all except for the dorm captain. When the young Nero opened his eyes, it was with shrill cries of fury and disgust. The other end of the dorm looked and smelt like a flooded public toilet. On top of this, he discovered that two fearful little boys had also wet their beds. Matron was sent for and glared at the felons as she stripped their mattresses. The rest of us looked on, thankful only to have avoided this ultimate humiliation.

But it did not stop there. After breakfast, we were marched to the washrooms and instructed to perform something called 'lavatory parade'. We did our best, while a teacher with a face like a guinea-pig, short legs and a very large bosom called Miss Hayes strode up and down to see we were properly engaged. One of us evidently miscalculated. We were lined up in the corridor so that under the direction of Obergruppenführer Hayes the school monitors, barely a year or two older than ourselves, could discover the noxious culprit. One by one, our waistbands were tugged open at the rear so that the monitor could peer inside our shorts and underpants. Eventually the poor little lad was discovered and led away. The rest of us felt both wretched for him and embarrassed for ourselves.

But this episode was also the beginning of a sense of solidarity. From then on, we the new boys were at war with them, the authorities, just as were the older boys. They quickly taught us the sign-language alphabet with which we could communicate secretly (and Old Georgians still can). In the absence of Harry Potter, books about World War 2 prisoners-of-war were favourite free-time reading.

Not that there was much free time. Academically St George's was rather a good school, pulling off the remarkable feat of teaching two different syllabuses alongside each other. In the mornings we did Spanish grammar, Argentine history, metric maths and southern cone geography (i.e. covering the area of South America below the Tropic of Capricorn). In the afternoons, with a break for football, softball or cricket, we did English grammar, European history, post-imperial geography, inches, feet, furlongs, gallons, pounds, shillings and pence. In the a.m. we referred to the Islas Malvinas and coloured them yellow. In the p.m. they were the Falklands, and we coloured them red. After supper we did prep in two languages.

Such an intense regime would surely be regarded as inhuman in 21st century Britain. But we took it in our stride, absorbing these parallel cultures without any sense of injustice. Children are conformists, and so long as our teachers, both Argentine and British, made it quite clear what was required of us, conform we did, at any rate scholastically.

Out of class, it was another story. Looking back, I can't

quite believe the anarchy that prevailed. The prep school bit of St George's catered for boys up to 11. Yet young as we were, our social lives were governed along the lines of Chicago mobsters. A new boy was quickly terrorised into pledging allegiance to one or another of several warring gangs. Their purpose was to build forts of sunbaked mud, fend off *Lord of the Flies*-style raids by rivals, and pursue fairly innocent sexual experimentation. One afternoon among the eucalyptus trees a rather fast boy called Copello showed members of the Blue Gang how to wank. We watched admiringly, but since Copello was only nine years old and there was no visible outcome to his actions, I remained puzzled as to their purpose for another two years.

The gangs also arranged escapes. These were quite serious undertakings, which involved digging under the tall wire fences that enclosed the school grounds. Beyond lay fields of thistles, dirt roads and the small suburban town of Quilmes, which had once been a popular dormitory town for British engineers brought over to build the railways but was now better known for its brewery. Minor escapes consisted of sorties beyond the wire to smoke Jockey Club cigarettes and buy ice-creams. But once or twice a term there would be more ambitious attempts to get away. Some heroes managed to elude capture for several days. They were invariably Argentine boys, unprepared for the harshness of boarding school life by early reading of *Stalky & Co* or Billy Bunter. At best they hoped that once they'd found their way home their distraught parents would remove them from the beastly place. At worst, there were famous precedents of fugitives being lavishly bribed with a Swiss watch or a Diana airgun to return to captivity.

Of course, those of us beginning to do Latin in preparation for an English common entrance exam should have realised the futility of all this. The St George's school motto is '*Vestigia nulla retrorsum*', which is usually rendered as 'No steps back'. Actually, the words have a rather more sinister ring in the original. They come from Horace's fable in which the clever Fox refuses to enter the den of the Lion because he notices that although there are the tracks of many creatures entering the carnivore's cavern, there are none leaving it. We had been warned.

Besides having a Latin motto, St George's strove very hard to run itself on the lines of a British public school in an Argentine setting. It was founded in 1898 with just six pupils but grew steadily. In 1911 a cricket pavilion was inaugurated to mark the coronation of George V. It is still there. The foundation stone of the chapel, where I was a treble in the choir, was laid in 1913. The first game of rugby was played in 1923. The prep school was added in 1929. The boys were divided into houses; there was a fine tuck shop; there were competitive games and an annual Gilbert and Sullivan. So much, so familiar to those with a knowledge of such institutions back in Britain.

But there were also unique features. Some were quite acceptable, such as the fact that since about half the pupils were Argentines, with no Anglo connection, we tended to speak Spanish, or at any rate Spanglish, out of class. On Sundays the school divided into Protestant chapel-goers and Catholics who attended Mass in the gym. Harder for the staff to deal with were the requirements of the Peronist government. We had to comply with various patriotic routines, such as the ceremonial hoisting of the Argentine flag every morning, accompanied by a song called 'High in the sky, the warrior eagle... this is the flag of my fatherland', and special assemblies, or *actos*, on days of national celebration which, as I have already observed, were numerous.

What happened on these occasions is that when we all stood to sing compulsory anthems with alluring titles such as 'We are the Peronist lads' and 'Students, let's raise the flag made illustrious by the predecessors of yesteryear', the entire school would join in a version of the words that was either politically subversive or mildly obscene, or both. Since some of the Argentine teachers were reputed to be government spies, this was actually quite dangerous – if not for us, then certainly for the headmaster and the English members of his staff. Not long before my time, a drunken teacher who had knocked over a bust of the Liberator had been jailed. Another, who had done something unmentionable with the flag, had been expelled from the country.

Our expat teachers during the four years I spent at St George's were pretty good. I look back on some of them fondly, especially the wise and kindly Irishman who was our choir-master and taught me the recorder. Mr Fremery Gahan was tall, thin and awkward, with a girlish mop of curly hair. Stalking around the school like a ganglier version of Jacques Tati, he was well aware he was a figure of fun but didn't mind a scrap. What made him popular with the boys he taught was a virtue rare among schoolmasters: he took his pupils much more seriously than he did himself.

Officially, there was no corporal punishment at St George's, since it was against the law of the land. This was fortunate for Mr Porter, a plump, choleric teacher who joined the staff accompanied by rumours that he had been sacked from several English schools for over-zealous beating. In Argentina his record did not debar him from a job, as the cane was illegal. But we watched him closely, secretly hoping the temptation would be too much and one day he'd go berserk with a cricket stump.

Unofficially, however, corporal punishment in the senior school was endemic. It was entirely in the hands of the prefects, who behaved with all the viciousness of teenage boys given unlimited power over their juniors. Inexcusably, the staff feigned not to notice what was going on. A slap in the face was regarded as a routine chastisement. More feared was something called Punishment Drill which took place weekly in the gym. It involved methods of inflicting pain and degradation which would have impressed Abu Ghraib interrogators. Boys would be made to stand in crucifix position holding a heavy dictionary in each hand until they could bear it no longer. When their arms dropped they would be slapped and kneed back into position. In a refined version of this technique one was ordered to crouch instead of stand, so that the back and legs suffered as well as the arms.

The gym's climbing ropes were a handy instrument of torture. Boys would be made to hang from them using only their hands for minutes on end, until they fell to the floor.

Then they were bullied back again. Something called 'drilling for oil' was another favourite with these sadists. The victim had to place an index finger on a mark chalked on the gym floor, then walk round and round bent double. After a while the dizziness and pain would be extreme and he'd topple over, only to be set back on his feet and forced to drill some more.

A caning would have been preferable to an hour of this sort of treatment. Why we didn't complain to our parents, if not the teachers, is hard to explain, except that some of these torturers were also great swells, boys we looked up to, heroes of the rugby field, stars of *The Mikado* or *The Gondoliers*. What is more, our code of honour regarded sneaking as the worst sin in the book, on a par with breaching a Mafia vow of *omertà*.

On one occasion things did go too far. There had been a disturbance of some kind in my dormitory after lights out. The usual punishment would have required us all to stand beside our beds for an hour, which was bad enough for tired 12-year-olds. But this time the prefects singled out the culprits and, incredibly, bound their wrists to the scalding-hot central heating pipes. Appalled, the rest of us watched while the boys screamed and struggled to break free. After some minutes they were untied and sent moaning to their beds with blistered wrists. Perhaps someone braver than myself told the authorities, or maybe it was Sister, who had to treat the injuries next morning in the infirmary. At any rate, the word was that the perpetrators had been punished, though we never learnt how. The incident was hushed up.

When I looked back at St George's from the relative orderliness of my English public school, I sometimes missed the anarchy. Hearing my new classmates complain about the repulsive food we were given to eat, I impressed them with an account of how we'd dealt with the problem in Argentina: the entire school, prefects included, had simply gone on hunger strike, tipping every morsel of the day's lunch into waste bins, banging the tables, chanting slogans and refusing to leave the dining hall until the headmaster himself appeared, promising the kitchens should give us whatever it was we wanted, probably steak and chips.

The Great Tuck-Shop Raid was another tale that went down well. There had been a school showing of Jules Dassin's ingenious heist-movie *Rififi*. Two nights later a gang of boys coolly pulled off an identikit crime. They entered the tuck-shop through the roof, stole some money and helped themselves to heaps of sweets and other goodies which were clandestinely circulated around the school. I can't remember whether the police were called in. I think not, to avoid a scandal. The burglars were never caught.

The general air of lawlessness was probably useful in preparing Georgians for careers in Argentine politics and business. But what I chiefly remember is an abiding sense of anxiety outside the classroom, where the teachers' writ didn't run and the older boys held sway. When I left in 1958 to go to school in England it was with mixed feelings: misery at being exiled from my family and home, obviously; but also a great sense of relief at getting away from the place where I'd endured four insecure, not very happy years. The following

July there was a catastrophic fire which destroyed many of the college's original buildings. No one was hurt as, fortuitously, the winter holidays had just begun. But hearing the news, I naturally speculated that adolescent arsonists had done the job and felt a surge of joy.

Today St George's is a highly successful institution, having celebrated its centenary, added a day-school in the north of Buenos Aires (at which my eldest daughter taught in her gap year), greatly expanded its student numbers and gone co-ed. Floreat St George's. Had the international baccalaureate been on the syllabus then as it is now, had there been girls (girls!) around the place to civilise it, maybe I would have argued with my parents to be allowed to stay on. As it was, I set sail for England with my mother and my newish baby brother, Colin, full of trepidation, knowing that in a month or so's time they would be coming back, but that for me it was a one-way ticket. At 13, I had been sentenced to transportation – not to the colonies but to my parents' – not my – mother country.

I did my best to enjoy the three-week voyage, envying porpoises heading the other way. I was quite brave when the moment came for my mother to drop me at my new school in Oxfordshire and give me a last hug, after an agonising tea with the housemaster and his wife. But actually, I cursed my parents, bitterly and tearfully. It seemed to me I'd been abandoned. I was a castaway in a strange, cold land without a friend to turn to and only the stoicism learnt at St George's to help see me through.

Yet realists as children are, I soon adapted. Within days

I was pleased to find I was at least as well up on most sub-
jects as the other new boys, surprised that I outshone them
in English grammar, and not too dismayed to spy a whippy
bamboo cane hanging in the housemaster's study. At least
Punishment Drill was behind me. I would survive.

LUNFARDO

Many of the words in tango lyrics are unintelligible even to fluent Spanish-speakers if they are not *porteños*, i.e. natives of the port city of Buenos Aires. This is because they are in a slang called Lunfardo. Like the tango, its origins go back to the end of the 19th century when immigrants from all over Europe were struggling for survival in the poorer parts of town, speaking a babel of tongues. Spanish was the national language, but the criminal and pimping classes evolved a private linguistic code to baffle the authorities and distinguish themselves from straight society.

Lunfardo is not really a dialect, though it is sometimes treated as if it were, dictionaries and all. It is simply an underworld vocabulary, borrowing words from the different immigrant languages and twisting their meanings. For example, the Lunfardo for policeman is *cana*, from the French *canne*, a baton. *Fungo* and *polenta,* Italian for mushroom and cornmeal, in Lunfardo mean hat and physical strength. The Spanish for the colour brown, *marron*, comes to be anus. More pleasingly, *papirusa*, a pretty girl, derives from the fact that so many young immigrant women from Poland were smokers, and the Polish word for a cigarette was *papieros*.

Lunfardo academicians have a bigger challenge with the word *mango*, meaning money. Somewhat boldly, they trace its origins to Napoleon's decisive victory over the Austrians at the battle of Marengo in north-western Italy in 1800.

The suggestion is that Piedmontese gangsters in Buenos Aires would refer to ill-gotten gains as *marengo* – an easy win, like Bonaparte's. Over time, this was corrupted to *mango,* or as an American mobster might say, dough. Hmm.

As with all slang, there is a playful element, a favourite formation being simply to change the order of letters in a word. Thus *macho* becomes *choma*, the Lunfardo for a hotel of assignation is *telo* and even tango is transformed into *gotan.*

Over time, Lunfardo spread from the slums, especially among the young and hip. In the 1950s, my friends and I used Lunfardo words all the time, barely aware we were departing from classic Castilian. A sexy girl was a *mina* (derived either from the Italian for female, *femmina*, or the Spanish for a mine, in both the penetrative and explosive senses). A ciggie was a *pucho* (from indigenous Quechua). The word for a brothel, also a shambles, was *quilombo* (courtesy of African slaves), while a snotty kid was a *pibe*, short for *pebete* (which apparently came from Portuguese *pevete*, a snivelling or maybe smelly boy, which in turn came from Catalan *pevet*, meaning a smokery or incense burner – a puzzling etymology).

A smooth guy, a swell, was a *canchero*, which entered Lunfardo via the pampas gauchos. Borges promoted the idea that these fierce plainsmen's idea of a really good time was a knife-fight to the death. However, they also enjoyed friendlier contests, such as a game called *pato*, which means duck, accounts of which date back to the early 17th century. It was a brutal cross between basketball and polo, played by teams on horseback, but with a trussed dead duck or a quacking live one in a basket instead of a ball. These gaucho sports were conducted on a dirt pitch, or *cancha*. The winner was master of the arena, hence *canchero*. At St George's the Anglo-Argentine boys evolved their own contribution to Lunfardo, so that anyone or anything approved of was described as *canch*. My parents were mystified when I told them I'd bought a canch set of marbles for just a couple of mangos. The equivalent then would have been English prep school boys routinely conversing in Cockney rhyming slang.

Che: While in linguistic mode, I must add a note about this little word, so commonly used in Argentina that it was the obvious nickname for Ernesto Guevara among his Cuban guerrilla comrades. Addressing a friend in Spanish or Spanglish, we'd almost always start our sentences with it. '*Che*, do you want to come to the *cine* this afternoon?' '*Che*, here's the latest *Dinamita*: it's full of pictures of girls showing their *tetas*.' It's the equivalent of 'mate' in London or Australia, 'bro' or 'dude' in the US. *Che* is not Lunfardo. Nor can it be reliably traced to native Indian or European migrant sources. Apparently it's also common in Valencia, Spain, though that's another mystery. So *bueno, che*, that's all I have to say about *che*.

Lunfardo was no passport to acceptability at Radley College, Oxfordshire, where I had to learn a whole new slang. New boys were squits, masters dons, prefects pups and the lavatories were bogs. Clearing the dishes after the filthy meals, a lowly duty we had to do in turn, was known as bumming.

At the cry of 'faggable' the last squit to present himself would be set some menial task, such as warming the bog-seat for a pup by sitting on it bare-arsed. After four weeks of study we had to take the new boys' test, a public inter-rogation conducted at the speed of a *Mastermind* contest. Failure to answer such questions as 'Who are the Midgets?' (the school's youngest rugby xv) or 'What is a fenny?' (a junior sculling boat) resulted in general derision and a requirement to re-take the test until word-perfect.

Another difficulty to be overcome was the way I spoke. Until this point in my life I'd no idea I had a funny accent. Our English teacher, who had an acerbic wit, put me right.

'Who are you?'

'Grove, sir.'

'Explain yourself.'

'What do you mean, sir?'

'Tell us why you sound like a cross between a Punjabi and a Scotsman. What outlandish part of the world are you from?'

'Argentina, sir.'

'Well, Grrovv from Arrrgentina, you're the only foreigner in thees cluss, so if you're to make yourself understude we'll have to get you speaking like an Eenglishmun.'

Mr Ashcroft's mockery, quite a good imitation of an Anglo-Argie accent I guess, bore results. By the time I returned to Buenos Aires 15 months later I sounded posher than the Prince of Wales, arousing general mirth. Even my parents were a bit startled.

Once a year I flew back to Argentina for the Christmas holidays. This was thanks to BOAC's recently-inaugurated

Comet service to South America, which provided the first high-speed though costly alternative to making the journey by sea. Previously, children sent 'home' to be educated from Argentina were lucky to see their parents at all during their school careers. Even so, the Comet took over 24 hours to reach Buenos Aires, such was the number of stops it made en route. We came down in Paris, Madrid, Lisbon, Dakar, Recife, Rio and Montevideo before finally landing at Ezeiza airport. But this interrupted itinerary simply added to the excitement.

There were no in-flight movies, but who needed them? Apart from the long stretch across the Atlantic, we were no sooner taking off from one country than we'd be landing in another. Those were the days when airports were welcoming, uncrowded, even glamorous places. Each differed from the other, with shops selling native goods and agreeable bars where the local citizenry came on outings to drink cocktails and goggle at the jet-set. Best of all, our meals were not served in the air on plastic trays but on the ground, at linen-draped tables marked with little BOAC pennants. They were splendid affairs of several courses, fresh-cooked national dishes and free wine. It was at a breakfast in Rio that I tasted my first mango (in its non-Lunfardo meaning) and learnt that the locals spread their bread with mashed avocado, because butter went rancid in the heat. Instead of whizzing half-way round the globe in a state of semi-coma, we really did feel we were travelling.

It must have been horribly hard for my parents to send me, and later my two brothers, so far away from home at such a young age. Their unselfishness still amazes me. But the trauma for us was pretty searing too. The pattern of my life from 13 to 18 was different from any of my school contemporaries. Once I'd recovered from the aching home-sickness of my first term, Radley itself was fine. I didn't care for the cold showers before breakfast, the disgusting food, or being beaten by the headmaster for swearing during a chemistry class. ('Dr Cardwell tells me you said "Christ", Grove. That simply won't do. Bend over.') But such miseries were outweighed by good friends, excellent teaching, and lots of sport. We were on the playing fields or rowing on the Thames for a couple of hours every day except Sunday. Despite the tuck-shop, there were no problems with obesity. There was barely any free time to smoke a Woodbine behind the pavilion.

It was the holidays when I felt I didn't belong. My aunt and uncle in Weston-super-Mare provided a loving substitute for home. But Weston to me was one of the most dispiriting places on earth, not so much super mare as super mudflats when the tide was out. With its flaking hotels, dreary B&BS, its slot-machine pier and tacky souvenir shops, it was a seaside holiday town already in decline. Worse was the genteelness of the cardigan-wearing, Conservative-voting inhabitants on the one hand and the ghastliness of the day-trippers on the other. Architecturally, climatically, culturally, socially Weston summed up for me everything that was most depressing about England and the English.

There was, however, one aspect of my times in that seaside town which was totally thrilling and which I wouldn't

have encountered back on the River Plate. My cousin Penny
and I (we were nearly the same age) were both obsessed with
sailing. This obsession was based almost entirely on our being
avid readers of Arthur Ransome and of the Green Sailors
books by ex-submarine commander Gilbert Hackforth-
Jones. Apart from telling jolly good stories, especially in
the case of the creator of *Swallows and Amazons,* both these
authors were meticulous in the way they described the business of sailing small boats. The novels almost amounted to
instruction manuals. Neither Penny nor I, aged 14, had done
more than crew a dinghy once or twice in our lives, but as we
gazed across the Bristol Channel, we convinced ourselves that
we must somehow, anyhow, get a dinghy and sail her on those
muddy waters. My uncle and aunt gamely supported this
ambition. In nearby Clevedon we found a second-hand 12.5
foot racing dinghy called a Graduate. Pooling our savings and
with donations from other members of the family, we bought
the boat and my uncle trailered her back to the Weston sea-
front. On a blustery day, strapped into our Mae West RAF
surplus life-jackets, Penny and I launched our boat under the
trusting eyes of Uncle Gordon and Auntie Molly. We were
embarking on a terrifying act of deception. The adults
thought we knew what we were doing. We knew we didn't.
Neither of us had ever helmed a boat before. As the wind
caught the sails and nearly capsized us in our first minute at
sea, A. Ransome and G. Hackforth-Jones came to the rescue.
We hauled in the sheets, steadied the boat, and were soon
skimming away in a state of hysterical delight. Jib-booms and
bobstays, as Ransome's heroine Nancy Blackett would have

crowed. We survived. That first sail was the first of happy summers afloat, winters of sanding down and varnishing, and a lifelong enthusiasm for both of us. I've crewed in races at Cowes and across the Channel and for some years owned a vintage cruiser on the Thames. Penny still owns her own small yacht.

By the way, I've forgotten to mention the name of our boat. She was called *Ayacucho*. The previous owners could not explain this. But I, as a schoolboy student of the South American wars of independence, knew very well that this was the name of a famous rebel victory in 1824, under the generalship of Simon Bolivar. It led to the final shaking-off of the Spanish yoke from Peru and her southern neighbours, including Argentina. How a small wooden dinghy in Somerset came to be named after an historic battle on the far side of the world remains a mystery. To me, it was an enthralling coincidence, or maybe even kismet.

But despite the pleasures of sailing, or spells during the holidays when I went to stay with school-friends in more alluring parts of the country, I still yearned passionately for hot sun, big skies, the scent of jasmine and what I thought of as a looser, loucher, Latin way of life. I wanted to be riding a horse rather than a Raleigh bicycle, eating steak under the stars rather than beans on toast in front of *This Is Your Life*, hearing tango on the radio instead of *Housewives' Choice*.

Obviously, there was a good deal of self-pity in all this. My frustrations were probably much the same as those of any teenager pegged down by the conventions of 1950s Britain (which included, in my case, being forbidden to go to the cinema in a sleeveless pullover, which my aunt considered vulgar). The difference was that I had a focus for my resentments. I knew there *was* an alternative life I could be living, in an exotic country on the other side of the world where bronzed young people lounged beside swimming pools all day, partied all night and wore blue jeans without the disapproval of their aunts.

Naturally I erased from this Utopia all the bad stuff about Argentina. In 1955, an anti-aircraft battery had moved into the park opposite our flat. My parents kept the car full of petrol and packed suitcases in the hall ready for a quick flight. A military coup against Perón was expected any day and eventually came, the so-called Revolución Libertadora. There were not many dead, but 20 years later you could still see the bullet-holes and shrapnel scars in the walls of the Casa Rosada. Even with Perón in exile, the nation to which I'd so often pledged my childish allegiance remained mired in political corruption and unrest. It was divided by extremes of wealth and poverty. It was disfigured by pitiful shanty-towns with stinking open sewers. They were aptly known as *villas miserias*. One of them was the birthplace of Diego Maradona. In the countryside the corpses of dogs, cows, horses and, later, human beings were left rotting by the roadsides. Brutish police patrolled with pistols and machine-guns. Eternal sunshine? Had I forgotten the bleak grey winters at St George's, the summer nights (long before air conditioning) so asphyxiatingly hot one had to lie naked on a tiled floor to sleep? Of course. There was no place for these in my fool's paradise.

Yet for the next four years, a fool's paradise was what it

remained. This was because my annual visit to Argentina was always holiday time, eternal southern hemisphere high summer. It coincided with Christmas and New Year parties, and it was when the BA well-to-do would spend a fortnight on the chic beaches of Punta del Este, in neighbouring Uruguay. In such pleasurable circumstances, no wonder I invariably fell in love. No wonder I continued to see my South American homeland in a golden glow, suffused with aromas of BBQ and G & T.

I can see that part of the problem was the desire to seem a touch exotic to my English chums. I've almost grown out of that. But I do look back on my early childhood as enviably sunny, so much so that when my own children were growing up in London, I felt guilty they weren't having the same carefree, barefoot experiences I'd had, save for a few weeks each year in a rented villa by the Med.

Our summers lasted an eternity. The Argentine school year broke off for nearly four whole months, because of the heat. My mother, brothers and I emigrated from BA to our house in the semi-rural suburb of Hurlingham, 20 miles away, leaving Dad in town during the working week. From December to March we turned from uniformed schoolboys into subtropical versions of Just William: tanned, tow-headed, shoeless and unruly. The only time we put on our Green Flash tennis shoes was to play football, bicycle polo or cricket (about which more later). Most Hurlingham houses, however modest, had a pool or at least a round, corrugated-iron eyesore known as an Australian tank, fed by a creaking windmill. We spent at least half the day in the water.

Despite its being a British colony, Hurlingham could not easily be mistaken for William Brown's cosy village back in the south of England. For example, one's entrance into the town was marked by crossing a bridge from beneath which rose the most appalling smell you can possibly imagine. Whether the stench was of putrefying animals, chemical effluvium or human excrement one could not tell, as the barely-flowing goo below was too black to reveal its contents. Retching and laughing, we always chorused 'Ah, the Ponky Poo River!' as we drove over. It meant we were almost there, our Hurlingham home.

The house, not large but quite pretty, with mimosa and pepper trees in the garden, was on a dirt road. It became a quagmire in heavy rain. We were permanently at war with ants and mosquitos. Our main weapon was the Flit gun, a hand-held pump attached to a small round tank which puffed clouds of toxic insecticide into our bedrooms. This was in the days before DDT was banned worldwide. We were particularly wary of tarantulas, whose poisonous bite could supposedly kill a hen. I found an especially hairy one once on my brother's pillow, next to his sleeping head. I squashed it in a towel, with a very un-Indiana Jones-ish scream, warning Peter to watch out as tarantulas hunted in pairs. Behind our house, feral cockerels crowed with no regard to the time of day, while down the road there was a parrot called Pancho which sat at the top of a tree screeching *'Hijo de puta!'*, son of a whore, at anyone who came through the gate.

At the beginning of the holidays Peter, who was animal-mad, would be given a pair of rabbits or guinea-pigs as pets.

One summer it was a handsome brace of farmyard ducks. Donald and Daisy followed us everywhere, gobbling up slugs and pooing in the pool. The guinea-pigs were slain by the escaped Dobermanns from next door, but Peter was slow to accept the awful truth about why the rabbits and Donald and Daisy disappeared at the end of the summer, never to be seen again.

Also early on in the holidays came Christmas, another reminder that we were a long way from 'home'. But our elders did their best. After carols in the packed Anglican church, St Mark's, singing *In the Bleak Midwinter* in our shirt-sleeves, we'd race home to gather round the tree for presents. Our dad would preside, perspiring heavily in riding boots, red dressing-gown and cotton-wool whiskers stuck to his face with Pond's cold cream. The illusion was short-lived. As the sun beat down, Santa's beard would start to slip. The good old man would pant out something about watering his reindeers and disappear. We'd repair to the swimming pool for drinks and a dip. Then came the cold turkey, the potato salad, the coleslaw and the blessed absence of Brussels sprouts. Finally there was a token plum pudding, not much larger than a cricket ball and sold in aid of the British-American Benevolent Society. My younger brother Colin used to be commandeered to help mix the BABS pudding in an immense vat. He had to strip down to swimming trunks and tread the gloop like grapes. 'It was hard work, being up to my knees in the stuff,' he remembers, 'but good for rugby training.' The tiny pud would be paraded before us, complete with a sprig of artificial holly melting in the brandy-flames

– though what we actually ate was fruit salad and ice-cream.

The town of Hurlingham had grown up around the country club of the same name, founded in 1888 as a sporting and social venue for the British community. Inspired by the Hurlingham Club in Fulham, the Argentine offshoot became a much-loved institution for those who could afford the membership and us, their children. The club-house was a fine, sprawling, late-Victorian building. The bar had slowly-moving ceiling fans and served breath-taking *claritos*, the local dry martini. I can still hear the thwack of its mosquito-netted doors as members took their drinks out on the terrace. The dining room was famous for its lavish Sunday buffet and for a delicious dish called revuelto gramajo, consisting of fried julienne potatoes, scrambled eggs and ham. This was also the setting for summer dances. The music was always provided by Harold Mickey y Su Orquesta, the go-to band for Anglo-Argentine party-givers. They played fox-trots and sambas but, for reasons I've already touched on, never a tango.

REVUELTO GRAMAJO
For 6 people

This popular and simple dish was supposedly invented by a Sr Gramajo, an aide to the 19th century General (later President) Julio Argentino Roca, who led a campaign to 'extinguish, subdue or expel' the native Indians.

- 10–12 beaten eggs.
- An onion, chopped, plus a garlic clove, ditto.
- 400g very thin, crisp French fries, home cooked, or cooked from frozen. (You can cheat by using potato sticks, two 150g bags, to be found on supermarket shelves among the crisps.)
- 200g of chopped ham or shredded ham-hock.
- A cup of frozen peas.

Method
- In a frying pan, gently cook the onion and garlic with a little salt until nearly caramelised.
- Stir in the ham and the peas.
- Turn up the heat a bit and throw in the fries.
- Pour in the eggs and scramble gently with a spatula or wooden spoon. Season and serve while still moist.

The club's sporting facilities were terrific. There was a beautiful 18-hole golf course, five polo fields, stables for 250 horses, 18 tennis courts, a cricket field and a swimming pool. There was squash and a bowling green. Eat your heart out, Hurlingham sw6. Apart from the swimming pool, where I specialised in diving for Coke bottle tops, I did not shine in any of these pursuits. I tried to live up to my father's golfing expectations but spent most of the time replacing divots and flailing around in the rough. I was a complete duffer at cricket. Each summer a county player would come out from England to coach us in the nets, encouraging the beastliest bowlers to do their worst. I felt like a coconut in a shy. It was a torture I endured only to please my Pa. I played long-stop and 11th man for the Hurlingham Juniors, but I think I was in the team only because my Ma made flapjacks for the mid-match tea.

We rode a lot. My father made a deal with a crafty old gaucho called Merlo who stabled dozens of top polo ponies. For a discounted price, we boys exercised the ponies during the week, galloping all over the club grounds. We were unsupervised and I doubt if there was any insurance in place – for those very costly ponies, I mean. Did their owners know a bunch of kids were playing cops and robbers on their prized mounts, I wonder? At weekends Dad would lead us on long rides across the wild terrain of Campo de Mayo, a vast military base where the Argentine cavalry had its HQ. He had made friends with the colonel, who let us roam at will. There

Rhea

were hares to chase and the odd rhea, an emu-like bird that easily outran our horses. Lapwings rose as we forded the river, screaming *tero-tero*, which was the local name for the bird. The idea was to lead us away from their nests in the marshy ground. We never found one.

Here's an ironic story: my brother Peter, who became a keen show-jumper, was born in Argentina and therefore had to do military service at 18. Everyone dreaded the *colimba*, a notoriously rough rite of passage. The only way out of it was if you drew a very low number in the special lottery which, by some quirky tradition, exempted a few lucky souls each year. The Campo de Mayo colonel promised that when the time came, he'd see that Peter was posted to the cavalry so he could work on his jumping full-time. He might even make it onto the national squad. In consequence, Peter Grove was possibly the only person in the whole country who was actually looking forward to being called up. Cue Sod's Law: he drew the number 57 and never became a cavalryman.

The best riding, though, was in the camp. Have I mentioned the camp? That was what we called the countryside, *el campo*, whether the lush plains of the pampas, the craggy hills of Cordoba 450 miles north-west of Buenos Aires, or the huge sheep farms of the south. Every now and then our family would be invited to stay on a landowner friend's estancia. This was always a terrific adventure, involving enormously long drives on dirt roads across landscapes almost empty but for the occasional horseman or a gigantic *ombú* standing sentinel on the horizon.

The *ombú*, which belongs to the rare *Phytolacca* family,

is 'a very singular tree indeed', in the words of the much-loved naturalist and author W. H. Hudson. The small farm (close to where I went to school in Quilmes) where Hudson was born in 1841 was called The Twenty-five Ombú Trees, so he knew what he was talking about. In the magical memoir of his Argentine childhood, *Far Away and Long Ago*, he describes the *ombú*, which is really more a colossal herb than an ordinary tree, as having 'an immense girth – 40 or 50 feet in some cases; at the same time, the wood is so soft and spongy that it can be cut into with a knife, and is utterly unfit for firewood, for when cut up it refuses to die, but simply rots away like a ripe water-melon.' But the *ombú* had its uses: it served as a lofty landmark to the traveller on the great monotonous plains, and also afforded refreshing shade to man and horse

Ombu tree

in summer. And for our city-dwelling family, speeding across the pampas in a cloud of dust, *ombú*-spotting was our equivalent to I Spy With My Little Eye.

An especially thrilling visit to the camp involved loading our car onto an ancient steamer not unlike the Cotton Blossom in *Show Boat*. She chugged waveringly up the River Parana, frequently running aground on a mud-bank, while my mother, I rather fancy, stood by the stern-rail and sang *Can't Help Lovin' Dat Man*.

At the conclusion of these expeditions there'd be the estancia-house, typically a handsome, colonial-style building with a courtyard, a well, shady trees and a sprawl of stables. Many of the older estancias were established in the days when the hostility of the native Indians was a permanent danger. They still have an ivy-covered mirador or watch-tower to warn of raids, giving them an air of sturdy defensiveness as well as homely comfort.

The very grandest estancias in the country would rather sniff at the suggestion there was anything colonial about them. The rich, race-horse-owning families that built them in the second half of the 19th century seem often to have been of a romantic cast of mind. There is a sumptuous and costly book called *Estancias: The Great Houses and Ranchos of Argentina*, by Maria Saenz Quesada, where you will find Gothic castles, French châteaux, Tudorbethan manors, cloistered Spanish patios and Italianate façades. In the gorgeous photos, lawns roll, tiles gleam and once-red walls fade gracefully to pink and terracotta.

If the estancias we visited were a bit less grandiose,

they were always warmly welcoming. Aproned maids would lead us into cool, dark interiors furnished in heavy Spanish or English style. The lighting, powered by the estate's own generator, flickered. Once we'd washed off the dust of our long journey, our hosts would gather their guests on the veranda for evening drinks, which traditionally coincided with the daily news broadcast on the BBC World Service. Ice tinkled. The sun set. And unforgettably, through crackling airwaves, came the jaunty notes of *Lilliburlero*. Those were the days.

After breakfast came the day's ride, an experience very different from hacking in the home counties in a hard hat and jodhpurs. The sturdy pampas horses are called *criollos*. They are bred to go huge distances at a gentle, steady pace known as the *galope corto*. This is a smooth, lolloping half-canter, not unlike, come to think of it, the tango *caminita*. Over the saddle, to complete the rider's comfort, the peons would strap a big fluffy sheepskin. No hard hat, no jods; just espadrilles and jeans or the baggy gaucho trousers called *bombachas*. We'd ride for hours and hours across limitless unfenced grassland, astonished by the teeming birdlife, eyed by huge herds of Shorthorns and Herefords, whose grandsires had been brought from the UK to spread their beefy northern seed. Sometimes a chain would be stretched between two horses to put up hares for the dogs to course.

I seem to remember watching the gauchos lassoo calves and wrestle them to the ground so they could be castrated on the spot. They used the *facon*, the traditional gaucho eating-cum-fighting knife with an embossed silver handle, to do the deed. If the creature struggled, they clamped the testicles between their teeth to complete the operation... But just possibly this is a fancy of mine. I refer to what Hudson wrote in *Far Away and Long Ago*. He warns against the tricks of early memory, which are nothing but 'isolated spots or patches, brightly illumined and vividly seen, in the midst of a wide shrouded mental landscape.'

What's not fanciful is that the calves' juicy balls, lightly crisped over the embers, were among the prized delicacies at the barbecue lunches we enjoyed after the ride. Your proper Argentine *asado* is a meat-fest like no other. For a decent-sized estancia house-party two or even three whole lambs were crucified, roasted and basted for many hours over a glowing wood fire, begun at dawn. They were accompanied by every cut of beef a European butcher would recognize and some he wouldn't, from fillet and flank to stomach-lining and yards of intestine called *chinchulines*. There'd be kidneys and sweetbreads and chorizos and a hot, garlicky, vinegary sauce called *chimichurri*. It was a meat-eater's heaven, a vegetarian's hell.

CHIMICHURRI

Here is a basic recipe for this uncooked sauce which you can mix in a jar or bowl and adjust to taste until you reach peak pleasure. Some people add chopped coriander.

- 1 finely chopped red onion.
- 1 cup of finely chopped flat leaf parsley.
- 3 cloves of finely chopped garlic.
- 1 small de-seeded red chilli, finely chopped (or pinch of chilli flakes).

Lamb asado

- 1 tsp fresh chopped or dried oregano.
- 1 small cup of olive oil.
- 2 tbsp red wine vinegar.
- 1 tsp sea salt flakes.

Once a year the enterprising Anglo-Argentine Society here in the UK lays on a grand *asado* at a rugby club in London, around July 9th, Independence Day. The tables are well furnished with bottles of chimichurri. Old and new members of that distant southern community gather to share memories, avoid talking about the Falklands and eat the best meat cooked in the best way. But we've never had grilled gonads.

BALANCEO

As its name suggests, this is a tango step useful for gaining a sense of balance between the couple. You use it to pause or change direction on a crowded dance-floor. There is not much to it – a forwards and backwards movement, each longer step followed by a shorter, brushing the feet together in between. By this means the dancers may gently progress, hover in the same spot or by degrees perform a complete gyration.

I can't think of any other proper dance styles (I exclude the smooch, which is either improper or merely inept) that build in a respite of this kind. It is a manoeuvre that allows for both safe navigation and the collection of thoughts. In tango, the *balanceo* is a necessary skill. In life it is just as useful, though generally we don't get the hang of it until later on, after we've learnt the folly of not looking before we leap or failing to plan what to do after invading Iraq or Ukraine. Until experience kicks in, we are like novice ice-skaters, too frantic to pause: we keep moving, just so as not to fall down. So, inevitably, we fall down.

There is a connection between ice-skating and the tango, as it happens. In the early years of the 20th century, a period of enthusiastic entrepreneurialism, a splendid French-style building called the Palais de Glace was inaugurated in the centre of Buenos Aires, near the famous Recoleta cemetery where Evita lies buried in the family mausoleum. This was the grandest of ice-rinks. It had a round glass cupola, bars and cafés for the skaters and a subterranean zone housing the machinery that made the ice. For a time it was a great success. Folk who had never seen a snow-flake in their lives flocked there, strapped on clumsy iron skates and wobbled about trying to recreate the European winter scenes that hung nostalgically on their walls at home. Then the fad for skating waned. So the rink was superseded by a wooden floor, the ice-making cellars were abandoned to the spiders and the Palais was re-born – as a tango salon.

The year was 1915. The Palais de Glace was neither a brothel nor a dockside bar. It was a smart venue. Yet what the orchestra was playing was tango. The brave impresarios had taken a gamble that the risqué music and scandalous dance-steps of the lower classes were now sufficiently respectable to attract the bourgeoisie. And so they did. At the Palais de Glace, tango could be found for the first time in surroundings that didn't make you want to check your wallet after every number. The more daring elements of society poured through the doors and where once pleasure-seekers had teetered to find their balance on skates, now they did their *balanceos* in shoe-leather. The best bands played. Carlos Gardel sang. A poet of the city celebrated the Palais in excited verse: so lovely your atmosphere... 'tan lindo tu ambiente, tan *high life*, tan elegante'. But the attempt to make dirty dancing socially acceptable never quite succeeded. The low-life associations stuck. Happily for the image of tango, maybe, but not so for the Palais. The ex-ice-rink, ex-dance-hall was eventually closed down, refurbished and opened again in 1932

as an exhibition centre, which it still is. By the end of the 20th
century, the hall which had echoed to *The Skater's Waltz* and
La Cumparsita was putting on displays of Beatles photographs and Bob Marley memorabilia.

I learnt to ice-skate almost forty years before I tried to tango.
In Britain, it was the famously cold winter of 1962–3, the Big
Freeze, when temperatures stayed below zero for the whole of
January and February. I was in my last term at school, taking
entrance exams for Oxford, as one had to then. But the
ordeal of struggling through Latin papers and writing an
essay on the morality of euthanasia (this in order to read Eng.
Lit.) was greatly lightened by the fact that College Pond was
frozen. The pond was actually the size of a small lake and the
ice thick enough to bear the weight of the school car club's
Austin A30. Games were cancelled, the playing fields being
under a foot of snow. Boys cycled into Oxford to buy second-hand skates in junk shops. (Where have all the junk
shops gone? Gone to Oxfam every one. And old skates are
rarer than warming pans.) I borrowed mine from a friendly
master. We spent every spare minute on the pond. There were
bruising ice-hockey games using field-hockey sticks and a
shoe-polish tin for a puck. It was glorious.

So I found my balance on the ice and even learnt to go
backwards after a fashion (a skill with a tango-ish element,
I'd later discover). But as for *balanceo*, hardly. Reaching
the terminus of my school career was too exciting for sober
reflection. By the end of term I knew I'd got a university

place. The gap year hadn't been invented then, but I still had five months of dizzying freedom ahead of me. Each letter home outlined a new plan. I was to go hitch-hiking through Spain, learning French in France, driving to Greece. In the end, though, the notion of returning to Buenos Aires for a good long spell, even though it would mean a second winter, seemed not just alluring but important. My family was likely to stay in Argentina for many more years, if not for ever. Would I make my life there too after university, or stay in England? This visit might help me decide. Furthermore, so as to get a true measure of the huge distance that separated the two countries, I would go by sea.

The company my father worked for was not only in the meat business; it also owned the Blue Star Line, a splendid merchant fleet which traded all over the world. The Brazil, Paraguay, Uruguay and Argentina Stars were the four largest of their ships sailing the South American route. They carried 60 passengers as well as cargo. On the voyage to England, the holds were packed with chilled sides of beef, carcasses of Patagonian lamb and bananas loaded in Rio or Las Palmas. Outward-bound the ships carried general cargo, anything from Fordson tractors to Scotch whisky (an immense luxury in Argentina, where the local brew, called Old Smuggler, was made from concentrate and tasted of treacle). Sometimes on the northerly run there'd be a few polo ponies stabled in the stern well-deck, heading for Windsor or Cowdray Park, while a south-bound vessel might be carrying a prize Hereford bull, sent out to spread his vigorous gringo genes among the pampas-pampered herds.

My family, allowed back to England every three and a half years for 'home leave', loved these ships with a passion. Every 21-day voyage promised not just the fun of being afloat and visiting exotic ports-of-call, but also deck tennis, Puffed Wheat and high adventure. Things happened at sea which were altogether removed from our lives on land and, especially to us children, utterly enchanting. Our departures and arrivals were announced by thunderous siren-blasts from a Blue Star funnel the size of an office block. We were woken to the sound of sailors holy-stoning the wooden decks. A jolly steward brought tea and digestive biscuits. There were kippers for breakfast and sometimes fried flying fish which had foolishly crash-landed on deck during the night. At 11am cups of beef-tea came round. We watched whales blowing, porpoises gambolling under the ship's prow, and albatrosses hanging over our wake, waiting for the galley to tip its kitchen-waste over the side. Everyone had a daily bet on the number of nautical miles we'd cover by midnight. On reaching a new port we'd be greeted by the pilot launch, followed by a pair of tugs (in those pre-bow-thruster days) and finally a flotilla of bum-boats selling everything from maracas to macaws. In Madeira, boys dove for pennies thrown by the passengers on the top deck.

At the Sunday church service we sang *For Those in Peril on the Sea* in the forward lounge while the gigantic waves of a Biscay storm crashed over the windows and the pianist fought to bring his fingers down on the right notes. When the ship was pitching fore and aft in a big sea (as opposed to rolling, which is side to side: there were no stabilisers then) we children would sit on mats and slide up and down the long lino passages, whooping our heads off. An urgent series of short blasts on the ship's siren meant a boat drill. We'd race to our cabins to put on clumsy kapok life-jackets, then parade at our emergency stations. I was never sure whether it was a drill or the real thing. Even at a tender age I was suspicious enough of adult duplicity to wonder whether this time it really *was* abandon ship and we were being told it was a practice just to keep us calm. But this fear only added to the excitement.

Regular ship-board events were bingo, deck sports including cricket with a brine-hardened rope ball, horse-racing (using dice and model steeds) and a Crossing-the-Line ceremony when the tougher male passengers who had not traversed the Equator before were given a mock shave and dunked in the canvas swimming pool. Film-nights were held on the after-deck. We watched *Kind Hearts and Coronets* and *Ice Cold in Alex*, unforgettably enhanced by the sound of the sea hissing along the ship's side a few feet from where we sat.

Then there was the fancy dress party. I was invariably a pirate in gum-boots, striped pyjama trousers, an eye-patch and painted whiskers. The smell of burnt cork still makes me quiver with pleasure. My mother once went to great trouble to disguise herself as a lettuce, sewing a white dress with hundreds of leaves. As the evening progressed, they wilted and fell off, leaving her stained green and looking more like an asparagus. On a subsequent voyage, undeterred by this mishap, she returned to the vegetable theme, my brother Colin remembers. This time she posed as a cabbage, with an amusing caterpillar crawling out of her cleavage. An old boy noticed one of the leaves had detached itself, revealing her bosom. 'Madam,' he said, 'I fear your dumplings are boiling over.'

On one trip an elderly passenger died. This was Mr Pank, a florid old gentleman of Pickwickian popularity in the Anglo-Argentine community. He had taught me to row when I was a choir-boy at St George's and all the choristers had been rewarded for their efforts with a riperian picnic in the Tigre, a swampy delta debouching into the River Plate. I liked Mr Pank, who had not only shown me how to pull an oar but also let us little boys drink a few bottles of Quilmes beer. We agreed it tasted of bile, but pledged ourselves to persevere. The drama of his death eclipsed even that important memory. I'd have preferred his corpse to be slid over the side wreathed in a Union flag, with prayers from the Captain and cannon-balls at his feet to sink him. Instead he was kept chilled among sides of beef until we reached port. As soon as we had docked at Tilbury, a derrick winched his sheeted body over the side to a waiting ambulance, watched by the whole ship's company, so that it almost had the grandeur of a ceremony. What a way to go. I resolved when I grew up to join the Merchant Navy.

Now, April 1963, it occurred to me that if I could wangle a working passage, I had a chance to re-live all this. Such a thing was not unheard of. In those less bureaucratic times, adventurers could sometimes get a free trip to distant parts of the globe on a cargo-ship or tramp-steamer in exchange for unpaid sailoring. What's more, I had some pull with the Blue Star Line.

I called at the London headquarters. Summoning the spirit of Joseph Conrad, I put my case to a Mr Cox and a Mr Rae, mentioning my time as a leading seaman in the school naval cadet force (or farce, as our appalled commanding officer described my crew on minesweeper exercises off Portsmouth). No doubt my father had greased the rails, but it was still with a high sense of achievement that I left their office with a berth aboard the MV Scottish Star, sailing from Victoria Dock on 1 May, bound for Buenos Aires. Provided there were no objections from the powerful National Union of Seamen, I would be signed on as a passage-worker for the duration of the voyage. I must present myself no later than 10am on the day of departure.

It was a day I have not forgotten. From Victoria I had to get myself by tube to Plaistow, thence by taxi to the docks. Even if I'd known where to get one, I had far too much stuff for a seaman's kitbag. Having had to pack for five months away, I was burdened with two heavy suitcases (partly loaded with contraband Teacher's whisky for my father), an overnight bag filled with Milton and Wordsworth, prep for my forthcoming university studies, and a guitar. Desperately, I tried to persuade a porter to help me down to the District Line with my burdens. None would.

Eventually I reached the docks. I was in a state of physical and nervous exhaustion. In pouring rain I found my way to the Board of Trade office. Here I was to sign on as a bona fide seaman. A gauche 18-year-old public schoolboy among a throng of tattooed, hungover ruffians and dark-skinned Lascars, I'm still amazed I wasn't beaten up on the spot. (Lascar, by the way, was the general and unapologetically demeaning term for an Asian or Arab seaman in those un-woke times.) In my M & S anorak, burdened with baggage, I felt less like Joseph Conrad than Evelyn Waugh's William Boot, though mercifully minus the folding canoe.

It took several trips to haul my sodden luggage up the Scottish Star's narrow gangway. It was midday, two hours behind my appointed hour. But it scarcely mattered. There were no midshipmen to pipe me over the side – only an uncouth fellow who asked me my business and said he knew nothing about a supernumerary. He summoned the third officer, who checked with the second officer, who consulted the Mate. It was the first any of them had heard of a passage worker. And the Captain had not yet come aboard. Until he did, they treated me as a slightly superior stowaway. I was given a cabin and something to eat, but otherwise left alone. It was not the cheery fo'c'sle welcome I'd hoped for. To be described as a supernumerary is pretty devastating to the teenage ego. I fell asleep fully clothed.

At 2am sirens hooted, whistles blew and the gentle vibration of my bunk told me the ship's engines had started. I crept out on deck. We were slipping gingerly downstream between rows of vessels moored either side of the river. The skipper was on board, I concluded, and had decided not to leave me on the quayside. Nor had the seamen's union made me walk the plank. I was homeward bound.

We enter the world of working adulthood through different doors. Mine was not a door but a gate in the portside deckrail, from which I had to haul myself across a gap into a swinging lifeboat, suspended over the waves a few feet below. As soon as we left coastal waters and I had had my interview with the Captain I was ordered to mess with and work alongside the two officer-cadets on board. They were sturdy lads, my own age. One had been at Pangbourne, the Berkshire public school which in those days specialised in boys destined for the Merchant Navy; the other was from a grammar school. They were amiable enough, but I could see at once they'd lose no opportunity to put this Oxford undergraduate-to-be in his place.

That first morning the place they put me in was not comfortable. Hanging from the davits in a small open boat with a rough Channel sea running would be a bit alarming even if health and safety regulations had been invented by then. Which they hadn't. We had neither lifelines nor life-jackets, never mind a yellow vest and helmet. 'Not nervous are you, Trev?' taunted one of my companions as he made me lean over the side to check the handropes looped along the lifeboat's gunwales for waterlogged survivors to hang onto. 'Not a bit,' I shouted through the spray, whereupon one of the ropes I was testing parted in a puff of dust.

Our main task on the voyage, when not engaged in the mind-numbing chore of chipping paint, was to check and refurbish the four ship's lifeboats. From day one it was apparent they were in a shocking state. The emergency rations were rotten, the water-tanks half-empty and rusted through. The oars needed renewing, the sails mending. I planned to give my dad a roasting when we reached BA. Meantime, I was relieved to be able to prance about and tie knots as requested without giving the cadets a chance to sneer. And who knows, if the Scottish Star went down one day, my replenished barley sugars might even contribute to saving crewmen's lives.

The cadets had other tests for me. We were not a dry ship, but beer was rationed to a couple of cans a day. We saved up for a modest binge in their cabin. This was their chance to shock me with filthy postcards from Port Said, starring not only women with breasts as big as barrage balloons but also donkeys and Alsatians. I found them simply unbelievable and gave a worldly laugh. What did shock me rigid, however, were the photographs. I was not quite a virgin. I had lost my innocence a year or so earlier to an amiable nanny employed by the family who owned my father's company, who had generously invited me for a stay at their grand estate in the Highlands. The encounters were the more traumatic because of my terror that if we were discovered by my host creeping in and out of each other's beds, my father, back in Argentina, would probably be sacked. For this reason I went around wearing a jock-strap beneath my underpants beneath my rented tweed plus-fours, so as not to give anything away inadvertently. Well, the worst didn't happen, though it plainly wasn't the most confidence-inspiring start to my sex-life. It certainly hadn't prepared me for seeing actual close-ups of chaps – the very chaps I was having a drink with – in full flagrante with a pair of (as they rather curiously put it) bollock-naked women. I couldn't hide my awe. They were triumphant. 'Wait 'til Tenerife,' they chortled.

The ship was in ballast, no cargo, so our only stop was to

be a day and night at Tenerife to refuel. As we approached the island I began to fear a *Doctor At Sea* scenario with me in the Ian Carmichael role being hauled off to a brothel by sniggering shipmates. My anxiety increased when the ship's doctor for some reason invited me to sit in on his pre-docking surgery. This consisted of him sitting behind a desk and handing out small packages to the crewmen queueing to see him. What was in the packages, I asked innocently. 'Oh, the usual things,' said the doc. 'French letters, anti-septic cream.' I was impressed by how relaxed both he and his patients were about it all. Despite my Scottish experiences, I was still at an age or stage where lust and love were morally inseparable, at least in principle. Too much Eng. Lit.

Anyway, when the time came, I somehow managed to avoid being Shanghaied ashore. Perhaps I pleaded a head-ache. I spent the day in the company of the wireless officer, who was drinking gin and water. He astonished me by eating raw onions as if they were apples. I later learnt that this is a trait associated with alcoholism, though he never once offered me a drink. The cadets came back aboard bleary with booze and shiny-faced with sexual smugness. A few days after we'd been at sea on leaving the Canaries, the doctor once again invited me to attend his cabin. There was a much shorter queue this time, just half a dozen men. One by one they dropped their trousers so their genitals could be scru-tinised. The problem was crabs, a particularly virulent local strain, apparently. I could see them scuttling about amidst the pubic hair. The doc peered, probed and prescribed an ointment. My slight regret at not having ventured ashore diminished. Perhaps that's why the kindly medico had asked me along.

On our last night before reaching Buenos Aires, I was invited to a lower-deck party – no officers present or even cadets. I saved up beer to take along. It was pretty riotous. Much drinking and singing, my fingers bleeding from inept guitar strumming. Once again, as with the cadets, I had the uneasy feeling they were out to make a fool of me, a boss's boy bound for Oxford. Well, I was drunk right enough, but I wasn't sick and I didn't hit anyone or end up in a bunk with the gay steward who had a rose tattooed round his navel and had said 'Any time you want, I'll show you the stalk.' So I guess I survived. Not a moment of *balanceo*, exactly, but certainly a rite of passage.

GANCHO

Perhaps tango show programmes should contain a ciga-rette-style health warning: 'Some of these steps could seriously harm you and others around you.' What really excites audiences is the flashy footwork of scissoring legs and kicking heels, which appear to miss damaging vital parts by mere millimetres. It's true such manoeuvres are not welcome on the salon dance-floor. They require a bit of stage space to execute safely. On the other hand the basic *gancho*, which means hook, is not an act of violence: there is no actual kicking involved.

What happens is that one dancer, usually the leader, inserts a leg between his partner's just as she is in the middle of a backwards step. As intruding limb meets advancing thigh, sheer momentum impels the lower part of her leg to jack-knife, hooking itself sinuously round his. So what looks like, and indeed is, an interruption by one partner is trans-formed into an invitation to the other, with a harmonious outcome for both. It is another example of the way tango, while appearing to be a balance between aggression and sub-mission, is actually an act of mutual complicity.

I want to use the *gancho* as a metaphor for the extraordi-nary confrontation between Great Britain and what is now Argentina which took place more than two centuries ago.

I realise I'm straining it a bit, because extreme violence was indeed involved. But it did begin with what the British hoped would be an invitation or seduction. There were moments of complicity during the events that followed. And there was, at any rate in the eyes of Argentine historians, a wonderfully harmonious outcome which might not otherwise have come about. It took two to tango.

I'm talking about the Invasiones Inglesas, the English Invasions. In British annals, these distant events of 1806–7 barely merit a footnote. But in Argentine history, the Invasiones are a defining moment, the high-point of national glory. As a schoolboy I'd been taught to believe this wholeheartedly. The history of Argentina is so brief that the entire syllabus could be encompassed in a single academic year. So the same narrative was repeated in the classroom over and over again, with accumulating elaborations. We began with Columbus, jumped to the founding of Buenos Aires in 1535, then skipped briskly over the intervening centuries of colonialism to the English invasions, which led up to the war of independence and eventual freedom from the Spanish yoke on 9 July, 1816.

It all took place a bit over 200 years ago. We, the British, invaded and conquered. For a few brief weeks what we now know as Argentina belonged to His Majesty King George III. If we'd managed to stay put, another huge chunk of the world might have been coloured red in my childhood atlas. As it turned out, we suffered one of the most crushing humiliations in our military history. That's why the Invasiones Inglesas are as crucial to Argentina's sense of nationhood as the Armada and Trafalgar are to us. And that's also why, obviously, most Brits have never heard about it.

The fullest, best-written account in English did not appear until 2013, published by Pen & Sword. *The British Invasion of the River Plate, 1806–1807* by Ben Hughes is a superbly researched piece of work as well as a gripping narrative. What's more, its subtitle explains concisely why the significance of these events weighs so differently in our peoples' histories: *How the Redcoats Were Humbled and a Nation Was Born.*

With Ben Hughes's help, I shall tell the story of how this hazardous adventure on the far side of the world came to pass. In January 1806, a British expedition seized Cape Town from the Dutch. We wanted a secure port on the route to India. The Commodore of the fleet was an ambitious chap called Sir Home Popham, who had for some time been trying to persuade the Admiralty of the case for attacking the Spanish colony on the River Plate. Spain was in alliance with Napoleon, so disrupting the enemy's colonial trade while opening up a new market for British merchants was exactly in line with William Pitt's Blue Water Policy. This was a strategy for projecting power overseas by means of our all-powerful post-Trafalgar Royal Navy.

Popham was so bucked by the ease with which they'd taken Cape Town that his thoughts turned again to his River Plate plan. One day an American slave trader arrived at the Cape. This Captain Wayne confirmed that Buenos Aires was rich and ripe for the plucking, already resentful about its subservience to Madrid. That clinched it for Popham. Although

he had no official sanction, he was convinced Pitt would support him.

A fleet of five warships and 25 transports was provisioned
for the 4,500 mile voyage; and on 12 April a force of some
thousand men, including the 71st Highland Regiment,
began embarking. They were under the command of Brig-
General William Carr Beresford. He was fat, balding and
blind in one eye but otherwise, so it was said, an able military man. (He could not have guessed that a century and half
later his name would be so reviled in the land he was about to
invade that Mr Gahan, my favourite teacher at St George's in
the 1950s, nearly had a schoolboy riot on his hands when it
was discovered his middle name was Beresford.)

The evening before they sailed, Popham wrote to the
Admiralty explaining why he was disobeying orders, heading
off to South America instead of protecting the Cape from
French attack. He said he hoped that this project, 'promising
so much honour and prospects of advantage to the Empire,
will be considered preferable to allowing the squadron to
moulder away in a state of cold defensive inactivity.' He was
taking a tremendous risk. Success would make him a national
hero and no doubt enormously rich. But failure would mean
a court-martial, possibly even a firing squad, like Admiral
Byng after he lost Menorca in 1757.

Calling in at St Helena, the fleet picked up more soldiers
and was joined by three merchantmen. Originally bound for
Botany Bay, they decided their goods would fetch a higher
price in a newly-liberated Buenos Aires. That's real venture
capitalism for you.

On 24 June, having negotiated the treacherous shoals of the River Plate, the invaders dropped anchor in the shallows off Quilmes. This was the very place where 150 years later I'd be the not very happy St George's schoolboy I've already described. The school steeplechase course, which I remember with heavy-breathing horror, ran over the same swampy ground where more than 1,500 men came ashore next day. They immediately got bogged down and lost several cannon in the mud.

The British advanced on the city, astonished at the herds of wild cattle and horses, putting up coveys of partridge as they went. The resistance was scrappy. The Spanish troops were ill-disciplined, the local militias deliberately under-manned because of Madrid's fears of an uprising. By early afternoon on the 27th June, Buenos Aires had surrendered, the Viceroy had fled north with his family and the invaders were marching along the city's cobbled streets. The citizens hung out of their balconies to watch them pass. Among them was a pretty 20-year-old called Mariquita Sanchez de Thompson. She was the wife of the Captain of the Port of Buenos Aires, Martin Thompson, whose father had come out from England in 1750 and settled. Her maiden name was Maria Josepha Petrona de Todos Los Santos Sanchez de Velazco y Trillo. She must have been quite a catch.

Mariquita, who would become a leading salonnière and champion of education for women, wrote a vivid account of the invasions. That afternoon she saw the Scots of the 71st march past. 'The most handsome troops I had ever seen,' she recalled enthusiastically. 'They had boots tied up with latticed ribbons, a part of the bare leg showing, a short kilt, a beret with black feathers and a Scottish ribbon worn as a belt with a tartan shawl'.

The British Empire's newest acquisition was not a sophisticated place. The population was about 70,000, the dwellings mostly single-storey, the entertainments few. There was a theatre, a restaurant, a French pastry shop, a few cafés, several churches and hundreds of small groceries-cum-grogshops called *pulperias*. The tango had not yet been invented. According to Mariquita, the only distractions were 'praying and eating'.

So, obviously, there were opportunities here. The three merchantmen that had joined the expedition in St Helena quickly sold all their goods and made roaring profits. Popham wrote letters to the mayors of all the leading manufacturing towns in England, urging them to get busy exporting to the River Plate – and secretly ordering a great quantity of silk stockings for himself, having spotted an opportunity for personal enrichment among the Women of the River Plate.

Proclamations were issued. They promised freedom of religion, the lifting of trade restrictions and there was to be no order for slaves to be freed. All this was well received and many of the wealthier *porteños* opened their doors to the British officers: there were dinners and dances and even romances. On 19 July HMS Narcissus, crammed with booty, sailed for England carrying triumphant despatches to the Admiralty and a request for reinforcements.

But the British were being far too complacent; plotters

were already active. The more numerous were Spaniards loyal to King Carlos IV and the status quo. The smaller but very determined group did not want to swap one imperial master for another. They saw the situation as an opportunity to gain absolute independence from the Old World. A Frenchman called Santiago de Liniers emerged as leader of the irredentists, determined to take the country back from its imperial overlords. By early August he had collected a motley force of over 2,000 soldiers, militiamen and volunteers. Beresford could not get them to meet in open battle, where the superiority of the British troops would have been decisive. Instead he was forced on the defensive inside the city. Here it was Liniers' men who quickly gained the upper hand, blasting cannonades of grapeshot up the narrow streets, firing down from the rooftops, bottling up the redcoats in plazas and churches.

On the afternoon of 12 August, barely seven weeks after they had seized Buenos Aires, the British surrendered, many of them recording their deep sense of shame. As the men were led off to prison between two lines of ragged Spanish soldiers, one British officer observed: 'It appeared as if Liniers had selected this guard of honour from the dregs of his troops – to mortify us.'

With the prospect of British reinforcements arriving soon, the captured men and officers were quickly removed from Buenos Aires. They were sent into the interior and spread around villages in the pampas. For the next 12 months the officers would spend their time shooting, fishing and hunting rhea, the fleet-footed pampas emus which invariably got away. One group set up its own newspaper; another founded the first cricket club in South America. Some of the men chose to desert, find a wife and settle down.

Back in Britain, of course, none of this was yet known. The frigate Narcissus reached home on 12 September bringing the news of the latest addition to the Empire. The press and the populace went wild. Celebratory salvoes were fired in Hyde Park and at the Tower. A train of eight wagons laden with dollar coins, silver ingots and cowhides, each wagon emblazoned with the word TREASURE, was escorted up to London. Handkerchiefs were printed with portraits of Beresford and Popham. Meantime, Britain's manufacturing cities went into a frenzy. That winter, more than 100 merchant ships sailed for Buenos Aires loaded with all manner of goods, from calicos and cottons to snuffboxes and stockings. Early in October a fleet of seven warships and 25 transports sailed for the River Plate to consolidate His Majesty's newest possession.

Well, it was not to be. The reinforcements landed near what is now the fashionable Uruguayan beach resort of Punta del Este (where, as I've mentioned, I spent happy summer holidays) in January 1807. After bitter fighting, Montevideo was captured. In May, Lt General John Whitelocke arrived as the new Commander-in-Chief in the River Plate. His orders were to recapture Buenos Aires, but he was not to alienate the locals, the government clearly believing that the British would be welcomed as liberators. Where have we heard that before – the invited interruption, as in Iraq, Libya, Ukraine, as in the *gancho*?

Buenos Aires had plenty of time to prepare for what was coming. By early June Liniers had some 9,000 men under arms and in uniform. Native Indians, African slaves and even small children volunteered to fight. Food had been salted and pickled. Hospitals had been set up. Whitelocke landed his forces 30 miles away in marshy ground and appalling winter weather. It took them nearly a week to reach the city, harassed by bands of horsemen with lances and lassoos. The defenders planned to withdraw into the city and, as before, fight the invaders in the streets. Cobblestones were prised up to build barricades, cannon loaded with grapeshot were placed at key crossroads. The citizens were positioned on the rooftops armed with muskets, machetes and tubs filled with flammable pitch. I know all this because I drew the scene many times in my early history lessons. Our special heroines were the brawny-armed townswomen in flying shawls, pouring boiling oil on the redcoats, egged on by their cheering children.

Anyway, you'll have guessed the result of the Battle of Buenos Aires, which took place on 5th July 1807. Of the 6,000 British troops who took part in the vicious street fighting, 311 died, 57 officers and 622 men were wounded, 1,611 were taken prisoner. Liniers' losses were considerably lower. The surrender terms for the British to sign were, appropriately, written on an ass's skin. A midshipman aboard HMS Charwell wrote: 'A little army, composed of the finest troops in the world, to be worsted by a rabble... appeared to everyone incredible.'

Liniers threw a farewell dinner for his defeated opponents

in the same fort which had been the British headquarters just a year earlier. One of Whitelocke's aides recorded: 'The dinner was excellent. God Save the King was played. The healths of the kings of England and Spain drunk. Nothing exceeded the modesty and propriety of General Liniers.' Whitelocke, less graciously, complained about having been invited to dine with blackguards.

So that's pretty much the end of this seldom-told story. The last of the British troops left Buenos Aires on 12th July 1807. The prisoners of war who had spent the last year in the interior were freed and made their way to Montevideo to get a passage back to England, minus the hundreds of deserters who decided to stay put in the New World.

When the news reached England, *The Times* called it 'the greatest disaster that has been felt by this country since the commencement of the revolutionary war.' Whitelocke was court martialled. His trial went on for 31 days. He was found guilty of incompetence and surrendering unnecessarily. He was cashiered and declared totally unfit, though many, including *The Times*, thought he should have shared the fate of Admiral Byng and been shot.

Unbelievably, even as Whitelocke was being tried, plans were afoot for another invasion of the River Plate, to be led by Arthur Wellesley. But when Spain rose against Napoleon in May 1808 the idea was abandoned and the future Duke of Wellington soon found himself in the Peninsula, fighting alongside the former enemy.

Back in the River Plate, the consequences were also momentous. Heartened by their David and Goliath victory against Great Britain, the people of Buenos Aires began to believe they could shake off the Spanish shackles too. Oddly enough, a young captain in the 71st Highland Regiment, Samuel Pococke, had predicted this after Beresford's surrender in 1806: 'I am firmly of the opinion,' he wrote in his journal, 'that the 12th August 1806 will be the origin of the independence of this country. The seeds are sown, and before many years pass their production will be arrived at maturity. The Court of Spain will for ever lament both the conquest of Buenos Aires and the recapture by Liniers.' So it proved. On 25th May 1810, came the Declaration of Independence. Six years later, after a prolonged struggle – which Britain supported – independence from Spain was formally agreed.

So you could say that inadvertently, Britain helped set Argentina free from imperial oppression. You could also say that 175 years later another British invasion force did much the same again. When we recaptured the Falklands in 1982 we inadvertently spurred a disgusted Argentina to revolt against General Galtieri and thus set the country free from years of military oppression. And so it has remained. They've had some dodgy Presidents, yes. But not even a whiff of a military coup. Though of course schoolchildren are still colouring those islands yellow and calling them Las Malvinas.

So, after a fashion, I can say that my aggressive, submissive, ultimately harmonious metaphor isn't altogether out of place. It did take two to tango.

It is 1972. The invasion of the Falklands is ten years away, but there's enough trouble in the world to be getting on with. It's the year of Bloody Sunday, the Munich Olympics massacre and the Watergate break-in. I'm writing editorials about these events in the London *Evening Standard* (in those days an important newspaper, for which Londoners and commuters paid good money – 10p). In Buenos Aires, the economy is tanking. My father has been closing down the Vesteys' huge meat-packing business. Thousands of angry workers at the Frigorifico Anglo – slaughterers, flayers, gutters and carcass-strippers, not the mildest of men – have lost their jobs. (I remember scary occasions during my childhood when Dad had to confront mobs of strikers in blood-stained aprons, wielding their wicked knives.) Foreign businesses like Vesteys are prime targets for guerrilla groups, increasingly bold in their defiance of the military government. My father writes off-handedly that he is now varying his route to work and has a weekday bodyguard. The man is armed with a .22 pistol. I write back sounding like a worried parent: 'Things are getting dangerous. A .22 pistol is only one up from a pea-shooter. Shouldn't you and Mum be thinking of getting out?'

It was the middle of the night when the phone woke me. I can't now remember who was calling because at the word 'kidnap' I went into shock. It was probably Lord Vestey himself, my father's boss, the stupendously rich, preposterously young but thankfully level-headed Sam (31), at Eton allegedly known as 'Spam'. 'Your father... on his way to golf... alive and well, but...' I scarcely needed to listen. This was exactly as I'd feared it might be. The call ended on a

What the kidnapped man told his family...

NEWS ON CAMERA

I know I'm on the short list...

It's about the Honours List, Sir...

Suggest BLUE NUN Cranston, for services to The Community.

Blue Nun from SICHEL

KIDNAPPED — Ronald Grove, pictured at home in Buenos Aires with his wife, ex-actress Lesley Burton.

By PETER HARDY

London Evening Standard, Monday 11 December, 1972

reassuring note: the company would do whatever was necessary to get Ronnie released. But there was also a chilling instruction: I must not talk to the press. It was vital to keep the matter from the Argentine authorities.

This was a bit of a tall order for an ambitious young hack. On the tube into work I could see nearly all the dailies were leading on the story. 'British business chief kidnapped by guerrillas in Buenos Aires,' was the headline in *The Times* that morning, 11 December 1972. My own paper, the *Evening Standard*, would surely splash on it later in the day. And here was I, desperately anxious but with a unique inside track on the story, forbidden by my father's employers from talking to Fleet Street colleagues. Though of course, I knew they were right. The guerrillas had made it clear that if the police got involved, Señor Grove would be killed. This was no idle threat. Only months earlier a kidnapped Fiat executive, Oberdan Sallustro, had been murdered by his captors when the police came too close. They shot four bullets into him. But still, it was hard giving no-comment answers to the reporters, some of them friends, phoning me at all hours.

My editor at the *Standard*, Charles Wintour, was understanding. There was no pressure on me to contribute to the paper's coverage. Anyway, without much help from me the news desk produced a decent feature. It correctly reported that my family had lived in Buenos Aires for 27 years, that we had a 'bungalow' (well, we thought of it as a house) in the predominantly British suburb of Hurlingham, as well as a flat in the centre of town. The article explained that the political atmosphere in the country had become tense since a brief visit earlier that year by ex-President Perón, after a 17-year-exile in Madrid; and that the surge of nationalism this aroused encouraged the activities of various left-wing urban guerrilla groups, notably the Marxist ERP (People's

Revolutionary Army), the FAR (Revolutionary Armed Forces) and the Peronist Montoneros. Mr Grove knew he was 'on the short list' and had told his family he was a potential kidnap victim. There was a black and white photograph of my parents, which I must have provided. My mother would have been thrilled to be described in the caption as 'ex-actress Lesley Burton'. The last time she'd appeared on the professional stage was 35 years before (in *Housemaster* by Ian Hay, which ran for 662 performances at the Apollo, Shaftesbury Avenue – Mum's glory days).

Meantime, somewhere in a Buenos Aires suburb, in a stifling, low-ceilinged, strip-lit cellar, my father had been coming to terms with his predicament. His first note to my mother was dated the evening of his capture, Sunday 10 December. I have it in front of me now, written in a firm hand on rough paper, though I don't know how or when it reached her.

'Dearest Lesley: As you must know by now I was kidnapped on my way to golf. I was not hurt & I am being well looked after apart from being in a very confined space. They insist on no account should anyone inform the police. You must telephone Sam at once & tell him what has happened. When we were in London he promised to help quickly if anything like this occurred... Don't worry, darling. I'm OK, after the initial shock. Worst feature: I haven't got my glasses. Have just had a *bife*...'

He wrote to my mother again the following morning. He doesn't say he had any trouble sleeping, despite the terrors of the previous day. No doubt the steak supper helped, not to mention a few drams of Old Smuggler...

'I certainly never expected to be writing to you from this *carcel del pueblo* [people's prison] as these young people call it. The whole business was highly organised. I have someone in the cell the whole time – they have watches even through the night. It's not very nice not seeing daylight... It really is bad luck not having my glasses. They're going to try to buy me a magnifying glass today – it will make such a difference if I can read. I must say they try to get me anything I ask for within reason – even had a couple of local whiskies last night... These young people are all masked in *capuchas*, hoods with eye-holes, so I can't tell their ages, but I put them around 18–30. They are very polite and well-behaved – completely dedicated to their socialist views. I spent most of yesterday listening to their arguments, one at a time. Very intense...'

With his guards' say-so, my father began keeping a diary on the afternoon of his capture. He was driving himself to the Hurlingham Club for his regular Sunday morning golf game, he recorded. As he tried to pass a green van blocking the road, three men jumped in the car. One of them stuck a gun in his ribs. '*Es un secuestro*' – this is a kidnapping, they said, and pulled a pair of smoked glasses lined with cotton wool over his eyes.

After about half an hour, they transferred him to another car, later to a truck, where he was thrust to the floor with a blanket on top. Finally they stopped and he was led into a house where he was laid on a bed, examined by a doctor and given some sort of tranquilliser. A while later, he felt himself being manhandled down through a trap door, someone below guiding his feet onto the rungs of a ladder. When they took off the padded glasses, he found himself in a small cell about 8ft square, the ceiling just 3ins above his head. There was a bed at one end in a wire cage which they promised not to close if he behaved myself. 'I quickly promised.' That first night, and every night after that, one of the guards slept on the floor beside him.

The next morning he did exercises before breakfast and cleaned his cell. 'Washed at the basin and had to pot myself in front of the girl guard – not so pleasant but she took no notice,' he wrote, with admirable sang froid. 'Afterwards we played canasta on my bed.'

Back in London I carried on working, a distraction from the leaden fear I carried inside me. I kept thinking how horrible this must be for my mother, but couldn't call her even if I'd known where she was: I'd been warned her phone could be tapped by the guerrillas or the police or most likely both. This was more than a decade before the truly awful kidnappings of men like Terry Waite, Brian Keenan and John McCarthy in the Lebanon: they spent long years in captivity, while some of their fellow hostages were killed. Even so, I thought grimly of the ordeal of Geoffrey Jackson, the British ambassador to Uruguay, who'd spent eight months in the hands of Tupamaro guerrillas just the previous year, not to mention the recently murdered Sallustro. The particular horror for the relatives of a kidnap victim is that they are almost always third parties, helpless onlookers who only want one outcome, and at any cost. Despite daily calls from Vestey headquarters in Smithfield, there was no news, at least none they wished to share with me.

Wednesday 13 December. My father wrote another letter.

'Beloved: And so I enter the fourth day away from you...' He explains that his guards are members of a separate command (FAR) from those who did the actual kidnapping (ERP) and so are not aware of any details of what's happening outside. But they assure him negotiations are under way. 'They are extremely determined, kind, courteous... do their utmost to make me comfortable – even hot shaving water followed by eau-de-cologne. The doctor gave me another check last night and was very pleased with my physical condition – I do all the exercise I can within the space limits... I also now have a commode (what luxury!) instead of a pot...

'You'll be amused to know my nickname is El Lord. This morning my guard sent up a note by the communication cord reading as follows:

'"*El Lord apolilla como un duque. Asi que no despertarlo.*" [El Lord is sleeping like a duke, so don't wake him.] Am now being guarded by the 18-year-old señorita, who spent my siesta-time dismantling her machine gun... She slept here last night on a mattress on the floor, still hooded of course... long time since I slept with an

18-year-old. We will play canasta a little later... I forgot to mention an interesting example of their thoroughness: the guards don't know where they are. They also were brought here blindfolded and will stay until I go.'

Thursday 14 December.

'... Physically I'm in good shape. Dr came last night and said he was satisfied. Peculiar sensation being given the once-over by a doctor looking like a member of the Ku Klux Klan... It was so hot yesterday they sent out to buy me a pair of swimming shorts – very snazzy. They promised to let me keep them as a memento so that I can wear them on the beach at Punta del Este.' (He was astounded that his captors knew all about the family's new year holiday plans.)

Later in the letter there's an encouraging development:

'... whilst I was imbibing my pre-dinner Old Smuggler the senior guard came down with some news. He said further contacts had been made. Instructions had come from the action group handling the negotiations for me to nominate two men I can trust implicitly to act as couriers in handing over the money... I must not tell you their names but I'm sure they'll do their utmost to help. I wrote to both of them... apologised for mixing them up in this and telling them what to do and above all to keep absolutely secret... they know they are risking their lives if the police or army should get onto them...'

'The [Buenos Aires] Herald has just come; it mentions a
million dollar ransom. I hope it's not true... Whilst I am
writing my guard is making an exquisite little plasticine
bust of me. I hope I'll soon be able to show it to you.'

From the diary, Thursday night:

'My girl guard came down around 8pm with the stupendous news that agreement had been reached and if there
were no snags I should be out by Monday. I was so excited
I kissed her on her *capucha*. She was well insulated therefore. Nonetheless, she said she had a jealous boyfriend.
It would be too bad if I were to get shot before I got out...
Forgot to say they felt I must be tired of the FAR propaganda posters on the wall ("Perón is our only leader!")
so I asked if I could have some pictures of sun and sky.
They couldn't find any but proudly brought me a large
blown-up photo of Ché Guevara – not even smiling.
I've hung it on my wire bed-cage to shade me from the
guard's night-light. Ché fills this role remarkably well.'

The entry for Saturday 16 December shows a dismaying lack
of confidence in myself, or at any rate my profession.

'Newspaper says Trevor has come out here. Fine and won-
derful for Lesley, but I hope to goodness he won't try to
get mixed up in it. He just mustn't interfere. My captors
insist it would be fatal if press or police intrude at this
stage...'

Well, I'd already judged that my presence in Buenos Aires would be unwise, even if I'd been able to comfort my mother. But by then, unknown to me, she'd been secretly whisked out of the country to Vancouver, where my brother Peter lived. Presumably the Vesteys and the FO wanted her out of the way, now that negotiations with the kidnappers were moving to a climax. My younger brother Colin, who was then at Radley, waiting to break up for the Christmas holidays, recalls how he suddenly found himself being told to pack and prepare for a mysterious journey:

> 'A limousine collected me from school and took me to Bristol airport. There was a private jet waiting, just for me. We flew to Madrid's Barajas airport. There I saw a small, very frail-looking lady sitting by herself on a bench: my mother. We hugged each other for an age, with emotion and relief: we could now share the ordeal. She told me she'd been flown out of Buenos Aires with an old friend and employee of Dad's called Gerry Gowar. She posed as Mrs Gowar. Then I became a Gowar, too, and the three of us took off for Vancouver, travelling First Class...'

Down in his airless cell, my father was bitterly disappointed that Monday had arrived with no further news. But then they removed his watch. He was puzzled. The guards explained that they always did this prior to a release, to confuse any account the victim might later give the authorities. So it was a good sign. Later, a hooded man climbed down the ladder. The newcomer insisted that before he was freed, my father should submit to a lengthy interrogation about the Argentine meat trade. Having been assured this was not a condition of his release, but purely for the FAR's archives, he cautiously answered over an hour's well-informed, aggressive questioning. The interrogator returned the following day, Tuesday 19th. This time, however, he concluded the grilling with what might have been, beneath the hood, a smile: he told my father the ransom had been delivered. He would be freed that night.

I'm looking at the original of an alarming document: the kidnappers' typed instructions to Vesteys' chief Argentine lawyer detailing how the ransom is to be paid. At the outset, they insist on the importance of misleading the police and the press. There follow 11 numbered paragraphs explaining how two of my father's nominated couriers should drive out of Buenos Aires at 10am on Tuesday, each taking with him three suitcases filled with paper '*sin valor*' – without value. One should drive north to the city of Zarate, some 50 miles from the capital on the shores of the Parana River; the other must head for La Plata, 30 miles to the south-east. They should eat lunch at a local restaurant, looking expectant, then return home at 4pm. They were decoys. Meantime, the ransom money should be secretly transported to the actual 'designated intermediary', another of the hostage's nominees. The kidnappers suggest it could be hidden in one of the company's delivery vans. Should there be a problem with the Tuesday date, someone must go to the Opera café on the corner of Corrientes and Callao Streets in the centre of town, carrying a roll of red cardboard. He should stay there for exactly 15 minutes, from 8.30 to 8.45pm. In which case, operations would be postponed until the next day. The final paragraph is wonderfully assured: 'Don't be nervous; think and act calmly and all will be well.'

Thinking and acting calmly must have been appallingly hard for the real courier. He had to drive with the money to a certain bar in a *barrio* of Buenos Aires, following precise instructions as to route and speed. He had to park, leaving the engine running. He must then make his way to the Gents at the back of the bar, where he'd find a note hidden behind the cistern.

The problem was: there was no note. Nonplussed, he went back into the bar. The barman, who was watching, silently went into the lavatory himself and produced a slip of paper which had fallen down behind the pipes. 'Leave your car,' the note said. 'Get into the one you see parked outside. Leave the case with the ransom in your own car. Later on you'll hear from us how to recover it.' Which is what this very brave man did.

Back in the people's prison, word arrived that the ransom had been paid. The guerrillas were triumphant as they prepared to free their hostage. He was blindfolded and manhandled up the ladder, then carried to what he took to be a small truck. He was placed on the floor and covered in a rug. It was a hot night; he had difficulty breathing. After about an hour's drive, they stopped. The senior guard, the man whom the others called El Flaco (the thin one) and whom my father had come to like during their long conversations in the cell, led him from the vehicle. 'He told me it was 9.30pm,' my father later recalled, 'that I was in the district of Matanza and that within two blocks I would come to a paved road where I could catch a taxi. I asked for some money. He gave me 20 pesos. He told me to take off my blindfold and walk forward 30 paces without looking back. Before leaving me, El Flaco clapped me on the back and said: "Adiós. Go with God. Be proud of the way you have comported yourself. We have nothing against you personally".

After ten days underground, the moonlight and open air made the newly-freed prisoner feel dizzy. He feared he might seem drunk to the few people sitting on their stoops in the hot night. He asked a woman where he could find a taxi. 'There are no taxis here,' she said and showed him where to catch a bus. His captors had advised my father to head for the home of his friend Charles Lockwood, whom they had thoughtfully warned to expect a late-night visitor. An hour or so later, my father arrived at the Lockwood house in Hurlingham. He was driven straight to the British Embassy. It was 1am on Wednesday 20 December when he got there.

Later that morning a high court judge, acting with extraordinary speed, came to the embassy to receive my father's official 'denouncement' of his captors, without which he would not have been allowed to leave the country. In the afternoon there was a press conference, though by that time back in London, which was four hours ahead, the *Evening Standard*, my own paper, had already scooped the world: 'Kidnapped Briton is released for Christmas!'

That night, he boarded a plane for Vancouver. The *secuestro* was over. And so, in effect, was my father's career. He was coming up for retirement anyway and it was quickly

apparent that neither the Argentine nor British governments, nor the Vesteys, wanted him to stick around in
Buenos Aires, least of all in his snazzy shorts on the beach at
Punta del Este. He would have been a living advertisement
for the efficacy of the kidnapping business. After half a lifetime of living, working and raising a family there, he never
returned to Argentina.

Aftermath: Ronnie Grove arrived in Vancouver to a
joyful welcome and a cheerful press conference. I flew out
for a memorable family Christmas. The celebrations were
interrupted only by Mr Grove's having to attend hours of
debriefing by Canadian intelligence officers on behalf of the
UK government. This clearly gave him rather a thrill, which
was understandable. Speculation as to the amount of the
ransom remained just that: speculation. But the generally
accepted figure was a million dollars. Getting that amount of
currency into Argentina, secretly and in cash, must have been
tricky. The sum was equivalent to over $6 million in today's
money. The lessons were not lost on Argentina's criminal
fraternity, when they saw guerrillas getting rich. In the next
few years, 170 businessmen were kidnapped in Argentina
for increasingly large ransoms. One of them was my father's
friend Charles Lockwood, who had helped him on the night
of his release. Charles was kidnapped not once but twice.
In 1973 he was ransomed for $2 million. Kidnapped again
in 1975, he was rescued in a police shoot-out in which four
of his captors were killed and he himself got a bullet through
the leg. Several other members of his family were kidnapped.
One was murdered. After that, he wisely left the country.

It wasn't until a month after his release that my father discovered who had delivered the ransom. He wrote his colleague a gracious letter, expressing his gratitude and admiration for the man's courage. Quite rightly, he also thanked the man's wife for letting him undertake such a dangerous mission when many wives might have said keep out of it. But how different times were, when a letter of such a personal and heartfelt nature begins 'My dear Norris' and ends 'Sincerely, R.C. Grove'. No first names, no unstiffening of the upper lip.

Years later, I asked my friend Andrew Graham-Yooll, the courageous news editor of the *Buenos Aires Herald* during the years of the Dirty War, 1976–83, when the generals were in charge, what might have become of my father's kidnappers. Dad was especially anxious to know whether El Flaco could have survived the junta's purges. Andrew made inquiries. A senior FAR man, he was told, who could well have been involved in the Grove kidnap, had been captured and become a *desaparecido*. He had almost certainly been executed in the military's favourite fashion: flown out across the River Plate in a military aircraft, drugged, stripped and dropped into the sea.

I've no idea how long my parents might have stayed in Argentina had it not been for their involuntary departure. They didn't know, either. Finding themselves suddenly homeless in their sixties was a challenge. My mother would have preferred to settle cosily in England where two of her three sons and her brother lived. But my father was addicted to the sun and we could all see how unhappy he was at the prospect of English winters. Nevertheless, he gamely set off with his señora on a year-long search for Mon Repos.

They spent a month in Jersey, which might have been a clever compromise, but the rules for settling on the island were complicated and expensive. So they set off on a leisurely motoring tour of the Continent which eventually refined itself into a thorough exploration of northern and southern Spain. They sampled Barcelona and Bilbao and sent amusing postcards from a place called O Grove in Galicia. They paused in Cordoba and Seville, took ship to Mallorca and Tangier. But it was no surprise to any of us when the promised land turned out to be a secluded *urbanización* called Guadalmina, near the little town of San Pedro de Alcantara on the sun-blessed stretch of shoreline between Marbella and Gibraltar. Back in the 1970s the coast road was still only two-lane (known locally as the Highway of Death) and the developers had barely begun their depredations. At Villa Grove, my parents replicated their Hurlingham way of life with the bonus of the Mediterranean sea and Andalucian sierras. There was no need for Dad to drive to golf and risk being kidnapped on the way as a fine 18-hole course was just the other side of the hedge. My mother was able to resume her stage career thanks to an excellent am-dram society, in whose productions she often starred. The wine was cheap and Larios, the local gin, first rate.

So when I invited V, the *Evening Standard* colleague with whom I was falling in love, to join me at Villa Grove for a few

days in 1974 (I described her to my parents as 'a chum'), there
was little need to tell her about our Argentine background.
She could experience it first-hand. There was the pool,
the frosty G & T, the table laid for lunch outdoors. Fanny,
my parents' beloved maid, who had come over from Buenos
Aires to join them, greeted her with a hug: *'Ai, Señorita
Valerie, muchísimo gusto!'* That evening I'm sure we ate one
of Fanny's specialities, roast hake or coq au vin, and played
what we called the Acting Game, as we would have done
back in Hurlingham on a Saturday night. And while she slept
(chastely in the ironing cupboard), V was viciously bitten by
a mosquito, just as she might have been in Hurlingham any
night of the week. *Está en su casa*, as they say in Spain and
Argentina: you are in your own home. Next day, her bitten
eyelid was the size and colour of a Victoria plum.

She brushed this off, after being given an anti-histamine
injection by Dr Triay from Gibraltar. For the fact is that even
before I'd met her, V was already an ardent Hispanophile.
As soon as she set foot on Spanish soil, at 16, for a family holiday in Ibiza, she says, 'I knew that those scrubby brown hills,
as the flight landed, and the furnace-like heat that hit us on
the tarmac, were what I had always wanted. My sister and I
were both doing Spanish O-level and got plenty of practice
saying *"Debo ir con mi familia!"* repelling the importunate
Juanitos on the beach at Cala Bassa. I later went several times
to Andalucia, but never with such certainty as that summer
of 1974 when T came to meet me in Fuengirola, where my
newly-widowed mother had found a little house to retire
to...'

There followed several happy days. The Costa was very active socially back then, and not so downmarket as it later became. Locals included Sean Connery and Stanley Baker. George Brown, producer of *Where Eagles Dare*, was one of the first movie people to build a house there, with his darkly vivacious wife, Bettina. Their friends used to wonder whether their daughter, Tina, who was staying with them that week, would ever emerge from Bettina's shadow. (Just two years later, Tina told Valerie about her new love, Harry Evans.) 'Oh yes,' said Bettina, describing the social scene. 'We have parties all the time and we always dance like mad, the kaftans flapping away.'

What with the dancing and the tennis and the beach, it was not very surprising that when I took V out to supper one moonlit night at a restaurant called The Yellow Book, run by two charming gay Australians, I asked my chum off-handedly if... well, you can guess the rest. Once she'd been amicably divorced from her then husband, reader, I married her.

In 1982, ten years after my father's kidnap, Argentina seized the Falklands. I was working at the *Observer* and found myself dreadfully torn. I was revolted by the Galtieri government's cynical attempt to win popular support by invading the islands. But equally, I was worried for the safety of friends and distressed at the spectacle of my former countrymen being reviled as a nation of uncouth desperadoes. I wrote a couple of on-the-one-hand, on-the-other pieces. I warned that the skills of the Argentine air force pilots should not be underestimated, which proved prophetic. But once the task force landed and our reporters began filing, I was no longer a soul divided. The British soon showed themselves to be brave and determined, while the Argies were an ill-led conscript rabble. My friend and former colleague Max Hastings 'liberated' Port Stanley. (Later, I helped edit Max's and Simon Jenkins' joint book about the war.) I was relieved when the Argentines surrendered. I was delighted, as were most Argentines themselves, when the disgraced and defeated military junta subsequently fell.

Ten years after the Falklands war, in 1992, I was in the happy position of being editor of the *Sunday Telegraph*. I commissioned myself to write an anniversary article and caught a plane to Buenos Aires. I was especially curious to know what had become of the Anglo-Argentine community back in 1982 and now, a decade later. The answer, I discovered, was not very much. At the time of the invasion, there was no outbreak of panic. One or two firms, such as Lloyds Bank, shipped their staff over to Uruguay, out of harm's way. British-born teachers at my old school, St George's, were offered free flights to safety. But none of them left. For a while the London Grill became simply The Grill, then quickly changed back. If London's Hurlingham Club had been a nest of expat Argies during hostilities, it would probably have closed for the duration. At the very least it would have been daubed with graffiti of the 'Gotcha!' variety. But in Hurlingham, Argentina, calm prevailed. Anglo-Argentine residents were offered police protection in case of native hostility. But there was none. Some Anglos hung a blue and white Argentine flag by the front door as a precaution. A few Johns became overnight Juans. But instead of an explosion of Anglophobia, there were stories everywhere of locals coming round to reassure their English-speaking neighbours they were safe.

One of the people I interviewed in Buenos Aires was Alan Craig. He was a dark, intense-eyed young man who spoke with the authentic accent of Anglo-Argentina, i.e. like a South African who'd had elocution lessons from Manuel of *Fawlty Towers*. Alan's family had been in Argentina for generations. His grandfather won the DSO in the First World War. His father, Neale, volunteered in the second and returned to the UK to join the RAF. Alan was 18 at the time of the Falklands invasion. He had just completed his Argentine military service.

We met over a Coke in a downtown bar. 'At 1.30 in the morning a soldier brought an envelope to our house,' Alan told me. 'They were my call-up papers. My mother was in a state. I said "I'm not going." I still feel very British. But my father was firm. He said: "I don't want any deserters in the family." So I rejoined my regiment, the 7th Infantry, as an NCO.' For a month they dug in on Mount London and prepared for the British counter-attack. Another Anglo-Argentine, Michael Savage, was in his unit. 'By the time the British came we were starving, we were cold and we were wet. There were supplies coming from the mainland. But they got into the hands of people who *sold* them to the troops instead of distributing them. If you didn't have money, you didn't eat.'

When the attack came, they fought, then retreated. Had he killed any British soldiers, I asked. 'I was in charge of a mortar, so I suppose I could have.' But they surrendered fairly swiftly and were taken prisoner by the Paras. Alan's captors were astounded that he spoke English. They asked him to interpret, which he did, though he was frightened of being branded a spy. At this point something memorable happened: the wretched Argentine conscripts, who had been so ill-led and ill-treated by their own officers, found they were being decently fed and sheltered. Injured limbs were operated on instead of summarily amputated. Ten years on, I learnt, veterans of the debacle, poor boys from city slums and ill-educated lads from the interior who had never even seen the sea until they were dumped in Port Stanley or on the deck of the doomed cruiser Belgrano, were still making much of the contrast between their humane treatment as POWs and the national indifference to their plight after their return.

Michael Savage discovered that one of his captors was also called Michael Savage. Their mothers began a correspondence. Roberto Herrscher, another English-speaking conscript, learnt that he was fighting against a relative on the British side. He too found himself acting as an interpreter for his fellow prisoners and was equally scathing of his officers. Argentines would rather ignore the tenth anniversary, he said. 'We feel ashamed of losing the war and ashamed of being taken in by all the propaganda that we were winning it.'

It was pretty apparent there was more rancour among Argentines for their own former leaders than there was towards the British. Eric Henderson, an old friend of mine who ran a thriving PR company, was asked whether the British Hospital in Buenos Aires should change its name so as not to offend local sensibilities. The hospital, one of the best in the country, caters for all nationalities. 'Our market research showed the exact opposite,' Eric said. 'Everyone admired the efficiency with which the British recaptured the islands. Clearly, it was British-type treatment people wanted. We advised that the hospital's Britishness should be *emphasised*.'

So ten years on from Galtieri's cruel gamble, what had changed? The military rulers had expunged themselves. Democracy of a fairly stable kind was re-rooted. But the country, or at any rate its middle classes, remained disarmingly Anglophile. The Hurlingham Club still flourished. Argentines persisted in calling the Malvinas theirs, but it was the Kelpers (as the islanders were known) who still inhabited the Falklands. Nevertheless, I did detect a subtle difference among old friends and acquaintances. There was not so much talk of 'home'. No one planned to pack their children off to boarding schools in the UK. Few if any dreamed of retiring to a cottage in Sussex with roses round the door and the NHS down the lane. It was not just UK immigration policy to blame. The Falklands war made people look into their hearts: my impression was that most decided, faced with such a test of loyalties, they were a bit more Argentine than Anglo.

In 1993 I fulfilled a long-standing promise to take my wife and four children, ages 9–17, on a grand tour of my sunny homeland. Sunny, huh. During three weeks the sun shone on just three days. Most of Buenos Aires was flooded. *'Inundaciones!'* blared the headlines when we landed.: 'Thousands flee flooding River Plate.' All we could see of the Hurlingham club's famous polo fields were the goal posts poking above the water. There was a public service strike, making travel complicated (two taxis wherever we went). Our eldest daughter got locked in a hotel bathroom for three hours and then electrocuted herself. During a visit to our family's favourite estancia, my 9-year-old son's horse bolted and threw him off in a ball of dust. I galloped up to his motionless body, fancying buzzards circling overhead. He revived. A gaucho hauled him up onto his horse and

Oliver dressed as a mini-gaucho after tumbling off his horse

gently rode him back to the stables. As the nearest doctor was several leagues away, our resourceful hostess made splints for his damaged arm out of firewood and dressed him up as a mini-gaucho to cheer him up.

I decided we should cross the Andes on a bus. This would be more memorable than flying: and memorable it was. As we reached the frontier, the Paso Los Libertadores, at the highest point of the pass, we were suddenly engulfed in a roaring, blinding blizzard. Within a short time, the snow was knee-deep. In the Chilean customs house, motorists and bus passengers argued anxiously about what to do. Our drivers, Jorge and Carlos, were determined they would drive on down to Santiago. They were the only ones who did. Dressed in our summer clothes, with friends waiting for us in Chile, we boldly re-boarded the coach, along with a number of others. I helped put chains on the enormous tyres with glove-less hands. For several tense hours we slithered round icy hairpin bends, Jorge hanging from the door to yell to Carlos where the road ended and the precipice began. Thirteen hours after we had set off from Argentina, we rolled into Santiago, where the rain was falling so hard the whole city smelt of battered eucalyptus leaves. We later learnt from the newspapers that it had been one of the worst autumn storms anyone could remember. Ours was the only bus to make it down: everyone else was snowed-in at Los Libertadores for four days, living out of vending machines.

In Santiago I was mugged, not once but twice. To cheer ourselves up, we went to the cinema to see the film of Piers Paul Read's book *Alive!* It was the story of the Uruguayan

rugby team whose plane crashed in the Andes and whose survivors were driven to eat the flesh of their dead team-mates.
The children were enthralled. They began a lively debate
about which method of transport we should choose when
the time came to return to Argentina.

Having got us all safely home, I was in no hurry to return.
But the following year, I lost my job at the *Telegraph* and fate
took an unexpected turn. My former editor at the *Observer*,
Donald Trelford, rang. An Argentine entrepreneur who'd
made a fortune placing advertising supplements in newspapers around the world, including the *Observer*, had told
Donald he wanted to start a Sunday newspaper in his native
city in north-west Argentina, Tucumán. He was looking
for someone with editing experience to help him launch it.
Ideally, this person would know something about Sunday
papers and speak a bit of Spanish. Well, Donald knew I was
at a loose end and kindly thought of me: I fulfilled both cri-
teria, having been editor of the *Sunday Telegraph* and having
worked at the *Observer* before that. As for the lingo...

My Spanish was put to the test straight away when I
landed at Tucumán airport on a baking October afternoon.
There was a reception party of grave-looking young men in
the arrivals hall. One had a flamboyant pony-tail, two had
big moustaches. They advanced with outstretched hands
to greet the Señor Director, as they immediately addressed
me. They drove me into town, treating every word I said
with great reverence. Pretty rapidly, though, they began to

unbutton and by the time we reached my hotel, I was seriously alarmed about what I'd let myself in for. The owner wanted to launch the first issue of *El Periodico de Tucumán* in just three weeks' time, four sections, full colour. But as my new friends explained, they were short of staff, short of computers, the presses were 150 km away on appalling roads, and the designer from Madrid had not yet arrived. On top of this, Tucumán's long-standing newspaper, *La Gaceta*, founded in 1912, had made it plain it would be putting every obstacle it could in the way of the upstart newcomer, deterring our would-be advertisers and menacing our news vendors, if we had any. The chief reporter showed me a pistol in the glove compartment.

What followed was nearly two months of madness, mayhem and occasional merriment. I held on to my sanity (in those pre-email days) thanks to the fax machine. I wrote almost daily to Valerie and she to me, and sometimes to friends who were curious to know what had become of me. I think the best way to tell this tale is in extracts from those front-line despatches:

'This is a million miles from Fleet Street. *El Periodico's* HQ is a disused warehouse on a dirt road at the edge of town. Across the way is a prison with a mule tied to the gate. Cockerels, hens and chicks the size of crows patrol the fence. A pretty bitch puppy walked in here the other night off the streets and now lives under my desk. I removed her ticks with a cigarette. We are protected from thieves and journalistic rivals by gun-toting guards with torturers' faces. The weather is scalding. The flies love it. They are small and slow-moving, so get stuck in one's hair and ears. My steamy office is their favourite muster-station.'

'Trying to invent a new newspaper under these circs is exhausting. Key equipment is missing or broken, the phone system is catastrophic, there's no admin staff whatever, no envelopes, no stamps, no paper even. A general spirit of *mañana*-ism prevails. The photo library is a four-week-old copy of the *Sunday Times Magazine* and some tatty travel brochures. What makes all this tolerable is that the 18 people I have working with me, backed up by a quartet of Spanish journos who've come out to help, are highly resourceful and extraordinarily sweet-natured. They are geniuses with the Apple Macs, which they keep functioning with wires and string. One of them thinks he can download pictures from the French news agency AFP with an aerial he's made from a coat-hanger. The trouble is that knowing what genius improvisers they are robs them of the smallest sense of urgency. We have had four dummy print runs so far and the best we've managed was to miss the final deadline by two and a half hours! Dios mío.'

'... Today we learn from the owner whether we are to buy our own presses or continue to depend on the printers 150km away. You'd think with the planned launch date less than a fortnight off they'd have sorted this out months ago, but no one seems perturbed. Well, maybe they *can* transport three huge bits of machinery 1,000 miles from

Buenos Aires, bed them in, run printing tests, buy ump-
teen tons of newsprint, hire five more journos, set up
an ad sales department, buy six more screens, purchase
a scanner, build a photo lab, find a cartoonist and steal
La Gaceta's weather man (the only one in the province)
all before a week on Saturday. "Don't underestimate the
speed at which things move here," drawls the man I've
been waiting to see all day on a matter of extreme urgency.
I may take to chewing coca leaves.'

The team soldiers on.

'We work 14 hours a day, six days a week, never leaving
before midnight. Then we go for supper, which is fine for
Tucumános, who seldom go to bed before 3am anyway.
My preferred eaterie is one of the *empanada* shops, which
have tables and chairs on the pavements. The empanada is
Argentina's signature dish, but Tucumán claims to be its
birthplace. It is basically a savoury pasty, usually stuffed
with meat or chicken, packed with olives, eggs, spices and
sultanas. Chilli is optional. Some are made with cheese
instead of meat. Our favourite emporium is that of Doña
Sara Figueroa, who claims to be the national champio-
ness of the empanada. Doña Sara, a persuasive woman,
pins me in my chair to insist that the meat must be sliced,
not minced, so I let her see I'm putting that in my reporter's notebook.'

In actual fact, I lazily ignore her advice, as you will see from
the recipe below.

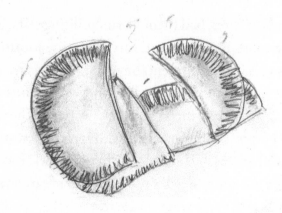

Empanadas

EMPANADAS CRIOLLAS

The key thing here is the dough. After many experiments, including chilled shop-bought pastry, I recommend the following, enough for 12–14 empanadas:

- Rub 50g cold butter, chopped small, into 250g plain flour until you have a sandy, crumbly mixture. Work in a beaten egg, half a tsp of salt, then add 90ml cold water. Knead into a smooth dough, wrap in clingfilm and leave in the fridge overnight.

You can have all manner of fillings. The tastiest is the one from Buenos Aires, which is much the same as the recipe I've already given for Argentine shepherd's pie. To recap:

1   In a spacious pan, gently fry two chopped medium onions in olive oil, with a sprinkling of salt, until almost caramelised.

2 Add 250g minced lamb or beef or a mixture of both and fry on a lowish heat, stirring regularly, until no longer giving off liquid.

3 Throw in 2/3 cloves of garlic, finely chopped or grated; a spoon of cumin seeds, lightly roasted; a good-sized cup of pitted green olives; and a can of chopped tomatoes.

4 Keep simmering and stirring. Unless you detest them, drop in a dozen cloves.

5 When the mixture appears cooked, not too dry and not too wet, and tastes fabulous, set aside to cool.

6 Mix in 4/6 chopped, hardboiled eggs. The filling is now ready.

Next, on a well-floured surface roll out the dough until not much thicker than a £1 coin. With a pastry cutter or inverted bowl, cut out as many discs, 10cm or so in diameter, as you can.

Put a teaspoon of the cold filling into the middle of each disc. Wet the edges and fold over, sealing them with a fork or, more stylishly, by pinching and twisting the edges between your thumb and forefinger. Brush each empanada with beaten egg and place in a pre-heated oven, 180–200°C, until golden – about 35–40 minutes.

Alternative fillings can be veggie (e.g. butternut squash, onion, sweetcorn, chopped tomato and feta, with perhaps a dash of cinnamon) or fishy (e.g. a tin of tuna, onion, chopped pepper, chopped tomato and sweetcorn, to which I add half a chopped apple for a touch of sweetness). Empanada bakers: get innovating!

'The hours around midnight are the best time to see the city, when everyone does a *paseo*, children included. By day, most of the place is an awful mess. There is disgracefully little of its colonial past left standing, despite Tucumán having been the country's chief city some years before Buenos Aires. Even the historic house where the declaration of independence from Spain was signed in 1816, which we had drawn so many times as schoolchildren, was pulled down. It had to be rebuilt to satisfy indignant patriotic pilgrims. The roads are dreadful and flood in the rains. Taxis, many without windscreen wipers, which makes them even more dangerous than usual, splash along like power boats. As for the trains, built and run so brilliantly by the Brits before Perón nationalised them, they have stopped running altogether and the tracks are now informal rubbish tips. The great sugar refineries and citrus plantations which once made Tucumán rich have shrunk or closed as world prices tumble. Many people, if they have any work at all, have more than one job. One of our reporters is a farmer, another a university don. Tough times in Tucumán, not exactly propitious for the launch of a Sunday paper. On the other hand, spring has arrived, the jacarandas are in blossom and I can now distinguish the three different cockerels that wake me every morning outside my hotel window.'

'The hotel, by the way, is supposed to be the best in town. My room is painted turd brown and has curtains made of rubber sheeting. I look out of the 6th floor window onto a swimming pool afloat with sodden newspapers and bobbing beer cans, but I reckon jumping into it would still be my best hope of escape in the event of fire. The hotel seethes with "congresses". Last night it hosted 1,200 moustachioed bus drivers and their 1,200 fat little wives. They danced to *Mac the Knife* in Spanish until four in the morning. The lobby is also a marketplace for skin-tight trousered lovelies, whose particulars you can browse over in a fully-illustrated album, available on request at Reception.'

By now we have an established office routine. 'We get in around nine. There is a hatch where we can get yerba mate or espressos, but no alcohol. The nearest thing to the Cat and Canary is a little bar down the road run, curiously, by the local automobile club. They have wine, beer by the litre and steaks. This is where the Señor Director takes his trusted lieutenants for lunch. The other day the patrón offered us chops, chicken or two and a half portions of roast meat. He left us to make up our minds, then reappeared grinning foolishly. "Señores, I am sorry to tell you there are now only two portions of roast meat. I have just eaten the half-portion myself."'

'Another example of untroubled Tucumánian demeanour: Paco, one of the Spaniards who's out here helping us, asked a pavement bootblack if he could deal with the blue leather shoes he was wearing. Certainly said the shoeshine and got to work. After a minute, Paco looked down to see the man was smearing on black polish. "What the hell are you doing?" shouted Paco. "Don't worry, Señor. I'm going to do the other one black, too, so they'll match perfectly."'

'Most of the locals have a strong element of Indian blood in their veins: coppery skins and hair as black as tar. But given the influx of Europeans over a couple of centuries, it is unwise

and also impolite to judge people by race or name. I'm introduced to a prize-winning, not very dark-skinned photogra-
pher called Font whom everybody knows as El Negro, and
a honey-coloured socialite called Negrita. Two of our own
contributors are Hugo Nicanor Splitz and Honoria Zelaya
de Nader. People in the news in today's *Gaceta* are Roberto
Lix Klett, Cristina Chalub de Merched, Atilio José Peluffo
and Maria Angelica Pitté Ford de Landa. Make of these won-
derful names what you will, but jump to no conclusions...'

'It's tiring keeping up my Spanish all day every day with my
colleagues. Still more demanding is having to give speeches
to local advertisers, do radio spots at short notice and interview strangers who just walk in off the streets asking for a job
(though I did discover our new illustrator this way, a fat boy
who popped in one morning unannounced and did a mar-
vellous caricature of President Aristide of Haiti with a few
flicks of his Biro). My other concern is trying to think up possible stories for our first issue, besides the failure of the sugar
cane harvest and the price of lemons. One hot topic is who
will be President Menem's running mate as VP in the next
general election. Should this post be offered to our own pro-
vincial governor, Palito ("little stick") Ortega, a former TV
crooner of questionable political talent, or to the governor
of Santa Fé, former racing driver Carlos Reutemann, talent
ditto? Meantime widespread official corruption, business
chicanery and presidential womanising (Menem: "I am not
a philanderer, I'm a seducer") earn hardly a shrug.'

'For the foreign pages the only possible subject seems to
be Charles and Diana, thanks to Jonathan Dimbleby's new

biography of the prince, which has been widely reported locally. My colleagues are sure I should write the inside story, confirming that Laidi Di is the reincarnation of the saintly Evita and Principe Carlos is a snob and a poofter. This would be a world scoop for *El Periodico*, they insist.'

In retrospect, I should have commissioned Mrs Grove to write a gossipy piece on the subject. Her faxed bulletins from home were exhausting. As well as doing interviews for *The Times*, finishing her biography of *The Hundred and One Dalmatians* author Dodie Smith and supervising four teenagers, she was leading a manic social life: partying at the Pinters', playing tennis with man-of-the-moment Jonathan Dimbleby, receiving John Mortimer's proposal that he should be *El Periodico's* drama critic ('He's looking for new outlets'). What was everybody talking about? Dimbleby's book. When Condé Nast supremo Nicholas Coleridge gave a sympathy lunch for the Princess of Wales at Vogue House, Valerie was on his right, just two places away from sad-eyed Diana. That might have made a colourful piece for our paper.

In the absence of a royal scoop, I wondered whether sport might give us a story. 'Besides football, Tucumán is mad about rugby, introduced by Brit railwaymen in the early part of the last century. I watched a match played in 100 degree heat where tackled players bled like gladiators when they hit the sunbaked ground. Instead of the communal bath after the match, both teams jumped into the swimming pool, pink with blood, and sang lusty Argie rugby songs. Their themes never strayed far from "Your mother is a whore" and "Your sister is a whore". Hold the front page!'

Our first press day, Saturday 5 October. I was up until
5.30am while the owner got us to remake the Letters to the
Editor page so as to include good luck letters from his publishing pals overseas. Our chief lay-out man burst into tears.
I very nearly did the same. We had just two hours' sleep
before tottering back to the office, where a stage was being
erected and bunting hoisted in preparation for the launch
party. President Menem and the Archbishop of Tucumán
headed the stupendous guest-list. I had to brief the priest
who was to pronounce the official blessing, not an editorial
task I had ever previously undertaken.

'... By Saturday afternoon, I thought the game was up.
Everything was late. We were two hours behind the deadline
when the last pages were sent off. It started to rain, then pour.
While everyone else went off to change for the fiesta, I stayed
here in the office to write my speech. Water began to seep in
under the door, along with cigarette butts and bits of lavatory paper. Hordes of policemen arrived, looking menacing
in big black rain capes. At about 11pm *le tout* Tucumán came
splashing through the storm with brollies raised. They were
dressed to the nines, women in very short skirts, the men in
shiny suits. I wore a stripy blazer, having not known quite
what to pack on leaving London. I looked like the master of
ceremonies on a cruise ship instead of the Señor Director.
However, this Henley garb went down well and was considered *muy Inglés*.'

'President Menem didn't show up, but some 1,200 guests
witnessed Padre Miguel, right hand raised over the micro-
phone, give the new newspaper his solemn *bendición*.

Team triumph: the first ever edition of El Periodico de Tucumán

El Señor Director at the launch party

Governor Ortega, the foxy-faced ex-crooner, passed through the crowd like royalty, ringed by security men, kissing the women, embracing the men. It was a feudal scene. Then the governor, the owner and I were led up to the stage, where I was interminably introduced as one of the two or three key people in world journalism. I made my speech – and jolly well, too, considering that I had just had word of a disaster. The lorry bringing the newly-printed copies of the first-ever edition of *El Periodico* had been held up. A truck had rolled over in its path. Dirty tricks by the opposition? Who knows? I desperately played for time.'

'The Governor spoke, very generously, considering the unkind things he must have guessed we'd be writing about him. Cue cheers and applause, wine and whisky. The band got going and the dancing began. Out of nervous tension as much as drink, the Señor Director shimmied furiously, circled by locals who presumably found the sight of a per-spiring Englishman in a striped blazer jiving with a tucumana unusual.'

'At about 4am, word reached us that the overturned truck had been pushed aside, the paper was on its way and we'd managed to print 21,000 copies. Thank God. Thank you, Padre Miguel. At 7.30am we left the party and headed into town to watch people queueing – yes, queueing – to buy our paper. It was a sell-out.'

I wish someone at the Palace had tipped me off during my spell in Tucuman that there were plans for Princess Diana to visit Argentina the following year. It would have made a front page story for *El Periodico*. I could have won great kudos in the province by recounting how I once helped Laidi Di to bean salad at a royal buffet. Nevertheless, I was thrilled to be invited, on behalf of the *Daily Telegraph*, to join her press secretary, Geoff Crawford, when he went to Buenos Aires to prepare the way for her arrival in November 1995. It was to be a four-day 'private' trip, during which she was to visit charities and medical institutions in her queen of hearts role. What Mr Crawford and I could see at once was that her Argentine hosts hadn't the smallest idea what a frenzy a visit by Diana, private or otherwise, would cause. They hadn't experienced the royal rat-pack in full pursuit. It was a touch embarrassing to be the only journalist in the Crawford retinue, seeing as its chief purpose was to choreograph events so that my colleagues in the British press didn't ruin the whole show. When I chatted to the editors of *Gente* magazine, Argentina's mass-circulation version of *Hello!*, I made the same point. They were coolly telling me she might not even make the front cover, assessing her pulling power as somewhere between a supermodel and a TV chat-show host. I told them they were crazy. 'Once she starts making eyes at the cameras,' I said, remembering that the Stones' recent tour had left one fan dead and the nation in a state of hysteria, 'she'll be bigger than *los Rolling*.'

How right I was. On 20th November, Diana stunned the world with her *Panorama* interview, revealing the inside story of her marriage. Within hours she had set off for Argentina, astutely putting 7,000 miles of ocean between

herself and the furore. Poor Geoff Crawford resigned, having
been kept in the dark about it. But the Argentines went mad
for her. She brought them her sweetest smiles and bent her
head over sickly children. They embraced the beautiful,
wronged young woman in a rapturous welcome. President
Menem, self-proclaimed seducer, led her about, strutting
like a bantam cock. I bet he came very close to asking her to
tango.

That was my last journalistic assignment in Argentina.
But not my last visit. One day early in the new millennium,
as I have described elsewhere, my wife asked: how did I want
to mark my sixtieth year on earth? A few tango lessons, I sug-
gested, then a tango tour of Buenos Aires. What a woman.
Gamely she joined me in those classes above The Boston
Arms pub in Tufnell Park. Bravely, she encouraged me to
plan a trip to Argentina. I say bravely because, as the reader
will recall, V's first and only visit to my homeland, on that
rain-sodden, strike-stricken, blizzard-blasted family holiday
back in 1993, had driven her half-mad with fury and frustration. Only her new-found love of the tango could have overcome her earlier determination never to set foot in South
America again.

She recalls our initial tango lesson as unpromising. 'It was
clear from the first class with Biljana that we were absolutely terrible *tangoistas*. I was tentative and lumpen; Trevor
was tense and sweaty.' But, she reminds me, 'We persisted
in practising nightly after supper, around the island in the

kitchen, and almost came to blows. We resorted to hiring the
tennis club's aerobics-room, with its wall of mirrors, so that
we could see how clunkingly maladroit we were. We invited
the only couple we knew who shared our tango passion,
Philip Hood, artist, and his literary critic wife Susan Jeffreys.
The solidly grounded Philip and the snakily lithe Susan were
way ahead of us in accomplishment and tried to sort us out
in return for a jolly evening and a glass of wine. I insisted
on buying swishy skirts, though T pointed out that Biljana
always wore the baggiest *bombacha* trousers and still looked
fabulous. We watched, over and over, the Carlos Saura film
Tango, and Sally Potter's *The Tango Lesson*, and determined
that one summer night we too would move, like Sally and the
divine Pablo Veron, tripping and turning in tandem, in free-
style harmony along the banks of the Seine – or indeed the
River Plate.

'I may not ever achieve those *adornos* that the slim young
tangueras manage so effortlessly. But I am now addicted to
being led, and will succumb to whatever capricious, unpre-
dictable *giro* my *hombre* decides is our next step. I am hard-
wired now to react in a Pavlovian way to the distant wail of
the bandoneon. Even if we still glare in fury at a mis-step,
or tread on each other's toes, my heart races at the very sound,
and I sprint upstairs to the salon with seduction in mind.
I am in tango's thrall and wish we had started decades ago.
Luckily, in tango age does not matter: only *el corazón*, the
heart, and *el alma*, the soul.'

With hearts and souls prepared for action, we landed back
in Buenos Aires in March 2004. Our dancing was inadequate

Bespoke in Buenos Aires: a tango shoe takes shape

but our besottedness was complete. Our very first night we walked from our hotel to the Confiteria Ideal, the most venerable tango salon in the city. Beneath its peeling plaster cornices and nicotine-stained ceiling, under the gaze of gloomy waiters, we danced for three hours, trying to be as inconspicuous as possible among the smoothly-moving couples, aged 18 to 80. Over the next few nights we took taxis across town to visit other *milonga* venues – El Niño Bien, El Beso, Salon Canning – where I fear we cut no dash. One morning, having paid a visit to Evita's tomb in the nearby Recoleta cemetery, we returned to our hotel suite in time to greet a chic young woman with a measuring tape. V's recently acquired passion for tango music was matched only by her ditto adoration of tango shoes. Our visitor, Leonora, whose name we'd been given back in London, was famous for the beauty and comfort of her bespoke footwear. With a look of rapture on her face, Mrs Grove extended her feet for inspection and ordered two pairs, one black, the other black and red. They'd be delivered by the time we got back from the next stages of our trip: horse-riding in the Cordoba hills, then a flight across the Andes for a stay at the Santa Rita winery and a weekend with friends on the Pacific coast.

You may have guessed by now that everything Valerie found disgruntling about her previous visit to Argentina was this time pleasing her immeasurably. Her horse at the Estancia Los Potreros, run by the long-established Anglo-Argentine Begg family, was an amiable mount called Cara de Queso, Cheese Face. He took her cantering sure-footedly across the roughest terrain, through fields of clover, thistle, thyme and mint, releasing wild aromas as they rode. At the Chilean winery, we stayed in a 19th century colonial palazzo that had been the owners' family home, set among rose gardens, box walks, palms and pines. 'All is perfection,' cooed Mrs G in her diary, fondling a glass of gold-medal-winning Cab Sauv. When we got to our friends' beach-house at Zapallar, the ocean which had been invisible to us through the rain and fog in 1993 now sparkled in the sun, revealing colonies of seals. We scoffed shellfish and quaffed pisco sours on a blue and white terrace beneath a blue and white sky.

But still, we were pleased to get back to Buenos Aires, where Valerie's new shoes were waiting and we could sally forth to try them out at midnight *milongas*, hoping (I feared in vain) that by now this couple of gringos fitted in. Well maybe we did, a little better than before. Mrs G had always objected to my wearing my 'cold, hard, wiry' glasses on the dance-floor. 'No one else does,' she scolded, looking round the room, and she was right. I discovered, as we went past other tables, that on every single one lay a pair or two of specs. 'So they haven't all got 20/20 vision,' I murmured. I took the hint. By the time we left for home, we had much improved our cheek-to-cheek technique. And of course viewing the dance-floor through a myopic haze rendered all the women beautiful, and all the men dashing, however aged or portly they might be.

My family might object at this point that a myopic haze was my default setting when it came to all matters Argentine, on or off the dance-floor. Fair enough. We romantics tend to see what we want to see, specs or no specs. What I hadn't fully realised was that my children, too, had grown up under the Latin influence, which had distorted their vision not a little.

Our eldest daughter Lucy, for example, says that even as a child she shared my pleasure in 'warm tropic nights, Spanish burbling on the taxi radio, the smell of black tobacco on the breeze, the sound of cicadas' – if not in distant Argentina then on holidays in Spain. Her sister Emma says that having two grannies in Spain (my ma and ma-in-law both lived on the Costa when she was little) and a dad who cooked chorizo and paella (choreetho and pie-eyya, never choritzo or pie-ella) was quite confusing: 'Aged 11, I even wrote in a school essay that I was a quarter Spanish.'

Victoria suffered from the same delusion. 'I grew up

thinking lunch at 3pm and dinner at 10 o'clock were quite normal. The cry of 'A la mesa!', echoing my grandmother, would summon us to the table. Sometimes there was tango and faux Sevillanas in the kitchen (later, in my teenage years I'd spend every Friday salsa-ing at Ronnie Scott's)... It was actually quite crushing to discover, when I was about 12, that we didn't have any Argentine or Spanish blood in our veins.'

It was the same for Oliver, our youngest child: 'I recall growing up thinking I was part-Argentine... or part-Spanish. It was a sort of stolen heritage. "I'm a little bit Spanish and Argentine," I would say to class-mates. I've always been so proud of my father's connection to the country – I tell people he is Anglo-Argentine and then I see the listener give me a sideways glance on account of my blond hair. I quickly continue, "He didn't escape Nazi Germany via a ratline at the end of World War Two... Born in Wales, raised in South America". I swaggered into my first ever Spanish lesson at school almost convinced I was already fluent... to discover I had a perfect accent but no understanding of the perfect tense. It would be years before I gained the courage to try and learn the language properly and even then my confidence was unfounded. In Mexico City I amused a bar-lady by asking what time the bar pigs, instead of closes... *cerdo* as opposed to *cerrado*.'

What helped fuel this fantasy among my children was that their uncles, both born in Argentina, had never shaken off the links with their *patria*. My brother Peter, he who might once have been a cavalryman in the Argentine army, now lived in Canada where he flourished as a bilingual mediator and owned the biggest barbecue on Salt Spring Island, decorated with galloping horses. Brother Colin had married a beautiful Spanish señorita, raised in London, called Aurora. They lived in Madrid, where their son and daughter, my children's cousins, spoke Spanish as their mother-tongue.

It was Lucy who followed her Latin leanings most determinedly. She did Spanish A Level and a course at Salamanca. She spent part of her gap-year as a teaching assistant in my old school, St George's. That was not a great success, as she was distracted by 'achingly beautiful boys with impossibly black eyelashes'. But she did live with a welcoming family in the Tigre delta, my old chums the Hendersons, went rowing, picked avocados from the tree and drank white wine sangria known as *clerico*. 'That gave me a taste of the ideal life I'd like to live,' she decided. Decades later, she became a teacher in Madrid, where she now lives her ideal in a chic little flat in an exciting barrio. 'After eight years here, I still get a frisson ordering a beer from a very normal bartender in a very average neighbourhood bar. My Spanish is better [actually, it's fluent], the tomatoes taste amazing, the crickets sing on summer nights and there are lots of men with impossibly black eyelashes.' If she fancies a taste of Argentina, there's a place around the corner called Sabores Patagonicos which serves Malbec and empanadas.

Back here in London, Lucy's siblings still show signs of yearnings unfulfilled. 'I always thought,' says Victoria, 'I'd end up living in a Latin country, or at least one with a more tropical clime and fiesta vibes. I think we all did. What are we doing here?' Her brother Ollie lives in South

London, where there's a thriving Latino community. 'I still can't shake off my desire to be recognised as a fellow countryman. They play football opposite my house. I greet them with an "*Hola, buenos dias! Que te vaya bien!*" They just shrug and get back to their game. I sniff a chorizo like an expert, drink *yerba mate* from a gourd and listen to Willie Colon playing salsa. What a phoney I am. The identity crisis lies just beneath the surface.'

A touch more realistically, Emma says: 'I always mildly resented that we didn't grow up speaking Spanish in the house. It wasn't until I became a parent myself that I understood how tricky it would have been to "parent" in a second tongue.' She's probably right, though we might have tried a bit harder had I recalled that early in our marriage, Mrs Grove had taken clandestine Spanish lessons. In 1977, she decided it was high time she brushed up her O-level Spanish, got a book called *Conversaciones Españolas* and a set of Linguaphone records, paid our Spanish-speaking American neighbour, Nancy, £2 per hour and after 30 lessons, back at Villa Grove that summer, astonished the company by suddenly announcing: '*Soy la mujer la mas contenta del mundo, quizás?*' She might have thought herself maybe the world's most contented woman, but I'm sorry that, inspired by her example, we didn't try harder to propel our offspring along the bilingual path.

Perhaps that wouldn't really have changed things very much. In the last days of the Covid summer of 2020, our son Ollie married the delightful, olive-skinned, raven-haired Coco. At the masked, pared-down wedding he gave a very funny speech in which he enumerated the qualities he'd looked for in his future wife. On top of all these, he said, 'I wanted a girl who could drive and speak Spanish – Coco can drive and she *looks* Spanish... That will do.'

SALIDA

Five years had passed since my 60th year tango tour. Out of the blue came an invitation addressed to Sr y Sra Trevor Grove. My old girlfriend Jill, daughter of my father's great friend Charles Lockwood, wished us to attend the wedding of her son in Punta del Este, Uruguay. It would be a very grand affair, I knew. Well, Sra Grove and I thought: why not? We could spend some time in Argentina first. Valerie dug out her tango shoes.

It was December, 2009. There weren't many people in Buenos Aires we wanted to see. My dear childhood friend Camilo, whom my family had so fallen in love with during our visit in 1993, had been killed in a car crash. I only discovered this when ringing his home from our hotel to invite him for a drink, to be met with a long silence and a whispered explanation from his wife. I can't remember how I answered. Valerie says I groaned 'Oh no! Por Dios.' I do remember feeling sick and shaken: a prop had been knocked away from the edifice of my past. But at least there was Fanny, my parents' faithful maid, still chic and smooth-skinned at the age of 83. She had returned to Buenos Aires from Spain when my father died in 1980 and my mother returned to England, to spend most of her 25 years' widowhood in Henley. We took Fanny out to dinner and reminisced over *morcilla* black pudding and Malbec red wine.

And there was tango. We re-visited our favourite salons.

Leading role: my ex-actress mother puts me on a high horse

Still in the saddle: riding in the Cordoba hills

But somehow the magic had been tarnished. The Confiteria Ideal seemed peelier and more dilapidated than ever. The gloomy waiters gloomier still. There was even a crooner who broke in on the tango music to sing *My Way*. We took a taxi across town to find our favourite place, El Beso, closed. The late-night streets were deserted, apart from bands of sad looking people collecting cardboard and plastic bottles for recycling.

Down on the empty quaysides of the old port, whose barbecue restaurants we remembered wreathed in wood-smoke and thronged with jolly carnivores, we plodded through warm rain, being bitten by mosquitoes, looking for somewhere to lunch. The most dispiriting of these eateries was called Happening, where nothing was happening at all. There was no question: under the dismal presidency of Cristina Kirchner, Buenos Aires seemed to have become shabby and ashamed of itself. I felt the nostalgia that had affected so much of my life draining away.

A return to the Begg family's lovely Estancia Los Potreros in Cordoba to go riding again with Cheese Face raised our spirits. I had my favourite, a smooth-gaited Peruvian *paso* horse called Sol. Our legs encased in stiff leather chaps, we rode up crags, trotted down ravines, called in at the village school to greet the children and helped to herd the estancia's horses from their pastures to the corrals at sundown. We flew to Salta and Jujuy in the far north of the country, where some of the colonial past was still intact and we finally saw an Andean condor. To conclude our expeditions, there was the magnificent wedding in Uruguay which had triggered our journey in the first place. It was held in a luxurious rural hacienda where the Johnny Walker Black Label flowed, the banqueting was sumptuous and hundreds of beautiful bronzed young people danced until dawn. The band didn't play a tango. But then this wasn't Argentina. And even in Argentina, even in Buenos Aires, I had an inkling the tango was no longer the cultural glue it once had been.

A couple of days later, we were back in Buenos Aires to catch our flight to London. We took off from Ezeiza airport, scene of so many emotional farewells. Perhaps this, I thought, would be my very last goodbye.

Well, yes, maybe it's time for me to let go, Argentina, though for most of my life it would be true to say I never quite left you. I would like our relationship to have been a little closer, maybe a bit less Anglo, a shade more Argie, especially on the dance floor. At one of our last *milongas* in Buenos Aires, Mrs G and I had been tangoing rather stylishly, I thought. Then an elderly dancer who had been watching us tapped me on the shoulder and said, with a kindly smile: 'Señor, don't be afflicted. It takes a lifetime, you know.'

If only someone had taught me a little sooner, I might have been there by now.

END

It takes a lifetime. Painting by Colin Grove